Bible Verse Chants

Bible Based Chants
For Teaching English
As A Second Language

Glenda Reece

ISBN 978-0-9842813-0-5

Dedication

This book is dedicated to Ada Young, Lillian Isaacs and Leta Cornman. These three Bible loving Literacy Missions Christian women brought and kept me in this ministry by mentoring, guiding, helping and praying with and for me through triumphs and trials. They have continued to minister to innumerable people, even to the gates of Heaven.

So is my word that goes out from my mouth:
It will not return to me empty,
but will accomplish what I desire
and achieve the purpose for which I sent it.

Isaiah 55:11 NIV

Acknowledgments

Many people have contributed to my growth and understanding in teaching English to speakers of other languages. Each author, whose book I have used, has helped deepen my understanding and teaching ability. I appreciate the work of Judy Gilbert, Howard Woods, Donna Brinton, Robert Dixon, Elizabeth Clarey, Nina Weinstein, and Don and Eileen Nilson. Their books and presentations have been invaluable.

Carolyn Graham visited North Carolina in the early 1980s. Her first book, *Jazz Chants,* started me on chanting and teaching with chants. I have taught from all of her books and CDs and continue to do so. Her contributions to the field of English teaching are uncountable.

Thanks

Preston Reece, my husband, spent innumerable hours creating the *Rhythm of the Language* "bubbles", editing, formatting, making suggestions and getting it published. Without his diligence and love, this joint venture would never have come to pass.

About Chanting

Combining my desire to teach English and the Bible, I felt led to write a selection of Bible Verse Chants. Chanting is not new at all. Perhaps Jesus learned much of the Torah while chanting.*

Memorizing Bible verses can be difficult, and in addition it's almost old-fashioned. But when students chant, the memory work comes easier. For International students of English and of the Bible, chants offer lots of help in memorization as well as improving pronunciation and rhythm.

Chanting is fun, and that makes repetition more acceptable. Repetition is absolutely essential in memorization, so the more ways you find to repeat, the more fun the chant is, and the easier it is to memorize the verse. The *rule of five* (see page 11) is set up to move information from short-term memory to long-term memory. Just reading a verse once will not accomplish the goal of teaching clear pronunciation, Adding rhythm, and enthusiasm will help, and occasionally having a student be the leader will also help.

To chant, divide the class into two groups. Have group one read the first box labeled *Group 1*; then have the other group read the first box labeled *Group 2*. Continue with the following boxes and switch back and forth as indicated in the chant. All chants should be done quickly and naturally, using normal English rhythm. Chanting slowly is simply boring and throws off the rhythm of the language. Be careful not to make every word a content word when helping the student pronounce correctly. Make it delightfully challenging.

---

*"For the chant used in the mass today is a child of the chant that Christ would have heard in the Temple and synagogues. The early Christians neither composed commissions to revise the liturgy, not commissioned composers to recast the chant. They brought to the Christian liturgy the prayers and chants of the Jewish liturgy, and the style of music changed little during Christianity's catacomb years. Etheria, a Spanish nun on pilgrimage to the holy places in about 385, mentions hymns, psalms, responsories and antiphones as part of the Easter liturgy at Jerusalem, the first three being forms familiar from Jewish liturgy.

(Maternal Heart of Mary Community. http://www.aternalheart.org/library/chant_history.htm)

*"The (history of chanting) early development is difficult to trace because all the music was handed down as an oral tradition; nothing was written even though the repertoire for the Mass and the Divine Office comprised well over 2,000 pieces."

(St. Michael School of Theology. http://www.saintmeinrad.edu/monastry_lit_chanthistory.aspx.)

Contents

Section 1

Introduction

About This Book

Each Bible verse or short passage is one lesson; but it can be repeated if you feel the need. The intent of the book is to help students speak with the natural rhythm the way you would speak. That means speaking in sound units, and holding content words longer than structure words.

In the introduction, the book contains background material for the teacher. Some of this information is repeated in the lessons as a convenience, but also to be used as part of the lesson. The background material includes information about sound units, tone, rhythm, and stress. It describes content words, structure words, and focal words; and reminds the teacher of some teaching methods such as backward build-up, linking rules, and repetition using the *Rule of Five* described on page 11.

The lessons present Bible verses and use a variety of presentations to encourage students to participate and to learn the rhythm of the language by chanting and by reading material that provides visual cues such as different size bubbles and sound unit markers (forward slashes) inserted into the text.

Although the book is copyrighted, the owner of the book is granted permission to copy individual lessons for his/her own personal, noncommercial use in teaching the lessons as long as the copyright statement at the bottom of the page is included. No other copying, digitizing, storing, or reproduction of any type is allowed. The classes will be much more effective if each student has his/her own copy of the book. However, if it is not practical for each student to have their own book, you are encouraged to make copies from your book within the allowances of the copyright. The font used is intentionally large to enable use with overhead projectors.

The NIV Bible is used because it is easy to memorize and is recommended for second language students. The modern language easily transfers to the speaking of language used today.

In addition, since chants are fairly easy to write, this book should encourage teachers to write their own chants. Church based English programs promise to teach English, and I believe the promise must be kept. Bible verse chants do teach English. In addition, by teaching pronunciation rules you help student really learn how to apply the rules in all sentences.

Target Audience

This book is intended for use by ESL Teachers in church based programs. The Sound Units as illustrated in the book are intentionally made of short phrases so that beginner students can say them, but do not allow the sound units to prevent the proper flow of complete sentences.

Typographic Conventions

The following conventions are used throughout the book:

- Content words are **bold**

- Focal words are **<u>bold and underlined</u>**

- Linking is shown with underlining. Example: *and<u> it</u>* sounds like */andit/*

- Sound units are separated with a forward slash: sound unit 1 / sound unit 2 /

- In a few instances, a down slanting arrow ↘ is placed at the end of a sound unit as a reminder that the tone goes down at the end of most sound units and sentences. If you are a teacher, you may want to add many more.

Basic Concepts and Definitions

Sound Units

We speak English in sound units or with breath pauses. That means we avoid breaking apart natural units, like prepositional phrases, verb phrases, and short phrases in a series. A sound unit is one contained whole phrasal utterance with no breath to break it. It is frequently linked in sound, and could easily be mistaken for one word. Many sound units form natural phrasal patterns and are set off by commas. In normal speaking, all prepositional phrases are sound units, the verb in all its parts is a sound unit, and generally the entire subject with all the modifiers is a sound unit. Longer sentences break into sound units for comprehension and ease of reading aloud, and that is where the learner will pause half a second and take a quick breath, then continue. A good example of this is the last paragraph of the Gettysburg address where the sound units might be broken apart in this way:

> But in a larger sense / we cannot dedicate— / we cannot consecrate— /
> we cannot hallow this ground. / The brave men, / living and dead, /
> who struggled here, / have consecrated it / far above our poor power /
> to add or detract. / The world will little note, / nor long remember, /
> what we say here, / but can never forget / what they did here. / It is for
> us, / the living, / rather to be dedicated here / to the unfinished work /
> which they have, / thus far, / so nobly carried on. / It is rather for us / to
> be here dedicated / to the great task / remaining before us— / that from
> these honored dead / we take increased devotion / to that cause / for
> which they here / gave the last full measure of devotion— / that we
> here highly resolve / that these dead shall not have died in vain; / that
> this nation shall have a new birth of freedom; / and that this
> government / of the people, / by the people, / for the people / shall not
> perish / from the earth. /

Most native English speakers are unaware that we speak in sound units, but thinking about *The Pledge of Allegiance* and saying it aloud will help make the natural breaks obvious. Sound units are not exact; some native speakers will make longer sound units, and others will make shorter sound units. That is fine. We don't all mark the sound units exactly the same, nor speak them exactly the same. While teaching beginners however, it is better to use shorter sound units. As the teacher, you are the authority in the classroom. Depending on the level of your students, you should adjust the length of sound units on material you create for them. Most sound units in this book (but not all) are marked short enough for beginners.

Mark natural sound units as you feel appropriate for your students. Most short sentences are only one sound unit. For example, *Pick up the pencil. Hold that door!! Jesus wept.* would each be one sound unit. Ask students to count the sound units in a sentence. Encourage them to mark sound units in their books and handouts. Speaking in sound units is the key to being understood because that is what listeners expect.

Tone

Lower the tone of voice at the end of most sound units and sentences. Very few sentences in English go up in pitch (even questions). A very few of the Bible verses have illustrated this with a down slanting arrow ↘ but you may want to mark many more verses to emphasize this lowering of tone to your students.

English Is a Stressed Timed Language

(From *Rhythm and Unstress*, by Howard B. Woods)

English, typically, has a predetermined rhythm, and the syllables seem to scramble to accommodate this beat. The rhythm requires a major stressed syllable approximately every 0.6 seconds.

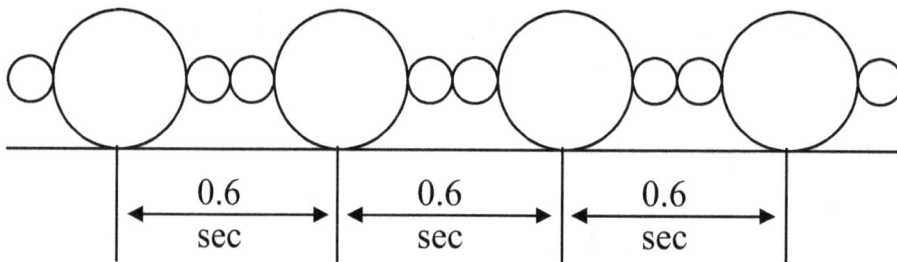

The rhythm of a typical English Sentence

The rhythm is maintained by stressed syllables. Any unstressed syllables are glided over rapidly and the stressed syllables are shortened to provide room for them.

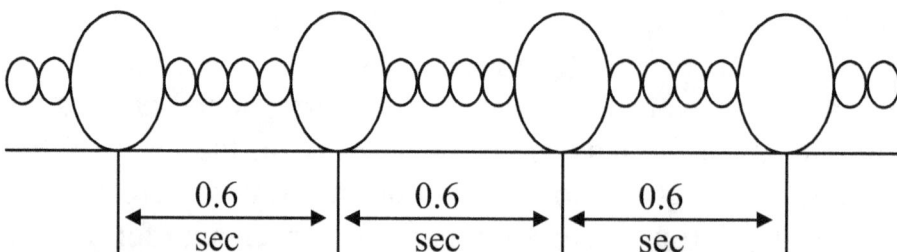

The rhythm with several unstressed syllables

If there are no unstressed syllables nearby, the stressed syllables are naturally lengthened in order to fill the spaces of 0.6 second intervals:

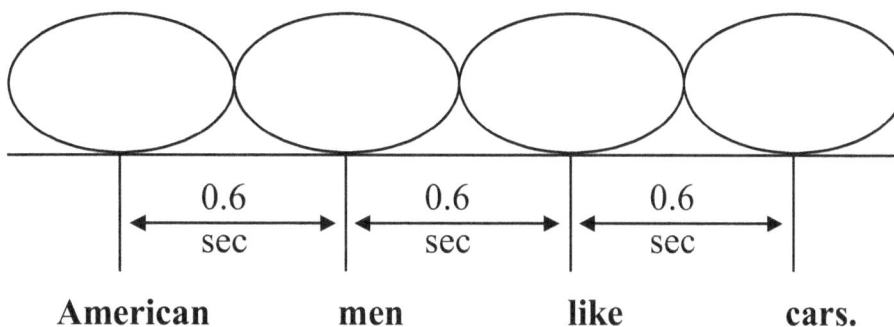

| American | men | like | cars. |

The rhythm with NO unstressed syllables

Long and Short Sentences May Require Equal Time.

Look at two sentences, which demonstrate the rhythm and stressed, timed features of the English language.

The cat is interested in protecting her kittens.

Large cars waste gas.

A native English speaker will rush over the unstressed syllables (structure words) so as to gain time for the full pronunciation of the stressed syllables thereby maintaining the rhythm. Liaison (linking) is in full swing wherever we find several unstressed syllables.

In pronouncing the second sentence, a native English speaker will prolong and stretch out the stressed syllables and produce less liaison in order to compensate for the lack of unstressed syllables thus filling the time gaps and maintaining the rhythm.

Content Words and Stress

Stress and content words are inseparable for me. Stress is length, not volume, and in English, as shown by Howard B. Woods, we hold the content words. We reduce the structure words to force the timing of the utterance. In this book, content words are often shown in **bold.**

Basically, content words are emphasized and held longer. Content words are all nouns (cat, person), all main verbs (sing, weep, hold), all adverbs (quickly, well), all adjectives (happy, white), and all question words (who, what, where, when and why, how) when used as question words rather than other ways in a sentence.

Judy Gilbert, Clear Speech, Ch. 12, 2nd Ed.

Structure words are the reduced or shortened sounds in English. These include the pronouns (I, we, you, yours), prepositions (in, of, because), articles (a, an, the), *to be* verbs, other auxiliary verbs (can, have, do, will), and conjunctions (but, and).

When content words are emphasized and structure words are de-emphasized, the contrast helps the listener to hear the important words.

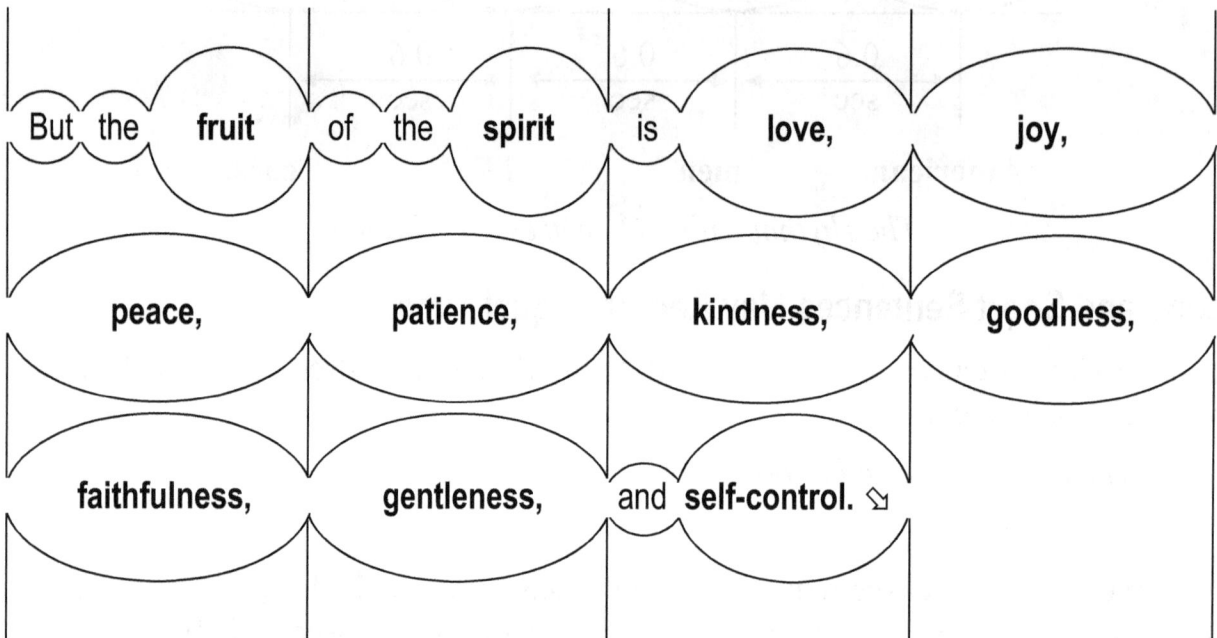

But the **fruit** of the **spirit** is **love,** **joy,**

peace, **patience,** **kindness,** **goodness,**

faithfulness, **gentleness,** and **self-control.** ↘

Focal Words

As speakers of English, we often add energy, excitement and importance to our words. Not every sentence has a focal word, but many do. In the sentence: *We hold these truths to be self-evident, that **all** men are created equal. All* is the focal word, and it is held a little longer like a content word, but it also goes up about half a step in pitch. This makes the melody of the language. The stressed word focuses the listener's attention, and therefore is called a *focal word.* Generally, the speaker chooses his own focus, and it can change with the speaker's emphasis. In this book, focal words are **bold and underlined.** Note however, that not all focal words are *content* words; *structure* words can be used as focal words also.

The focal word can shift, according to the meaning the speaker intends:

The **joy** of the Lord is my strength.
The joy of the **Lord** is my strength.
The joy of the Lord is **my** strength.
The joy of the Lord is my **strength**.

Backward Build-Up

Backward build-up is a technique to help the student with multi-syllable words. It is a good brain based learning trick. For example, the three-syllable word *blasphemy* can be taught by first saying the entire word, then holding up three fingers. Using the other hand, touch the first finger and say "me". Then touch two fingers and say "phe-me" (pronounce it like as you would in the whole word: say, "phuh-me", not "fee-me"). Finally, touch each of the three fingers in turn as you say, "blas-phe-me". A little practice makes this a very effective technique.

The Flap /d/ Rule

In North American English, the /t/ sound takes on a unique quality after either a vowel, an /r/, or an unstressed syllable. The tongue touches the tooth ridge very briefly, like a flap or a tap, and it is voiced. This sounds the same as when /d/ is found. There is little or no sound difference in words like *catty* and *caddy*. These flaps also occur in sentences and across word boundaries. *Part it on the side* sounds like *pardit on the side*. The Flap /d/ is found only in North American English.

The Linking Rules

Some simplified rules (from *Teaching Pronunciation*: Cambridge University Press).

1. Linking with /y/ or /w/ glides commonly occurs when one word or syllable ends in a tense vowel or diphthong and the next word or syllable begins with a vowel.

   Examples:
   Be able is pronounced *be* $^{(y)}$*able*. I won't *be* $^{(y)}$*able* to come over tonight.
   Create is pronounced *cre* $^{(y)}$*ate*

Also some words ending in /uw/, /ow/, or /aw/ add a (w)

   Examples:
   You are is pronounced *you* $^{(w)}$*are*
   How is it? Is pronounced *how* $^{(w)}$*is* $^{(z)}$*it?*
   flour is pronounced *flo* $^{(w)}$*ur* and *Do it* is pronounced *do* $^{(w)}$*it!*

Usually a word that ends in vowels moves smoothly to a following word that begins with a vowel.

Examples:
Bye, Oliver   *Anna eavesdrops*

2. When a word ending with a single consonant is followed by a word beginning with a vowel, the consonant is held and it sounds like it belongs to both words.

   Examples:
   That in sounds like *tha din* (the /t/ becomes a flap /d/ and is held)
   His arms = /Hizarms/, *Look at* = /Lookat/, *Mark and* = /Markan/
   Talk about = /Talkabout/

3. When a word or syllable ending in a consonant *cluster* is followed by a word/syllable beginning with a vowel, the final consonant is pronounced as if it belongs to both words/syllables.

   Examples:
   thrown out /nout/   *strong and* /gand/   *almost over* /tover/

4. When a word ends in a consonant sound and the next word begins with the same consonant sound, the sound is elongated, but never produced twice and no extra filler sound is used.

   Examples:
   eternal life   *its salty*   *good deeds*
   with this

5. The stops in English are t, d, p, k, g, and j. When a stop consonant is followed by another stop consonant in the next word, the first stop is not released and that helps the linking. The tongue is in the position but before the air is released the next sound is formed.

   Examples:
   and tell   *back pack*   *not good*
   bed post   *not just*

6. When a word ends in a /t/ sound, and the following word is either you, your, or you're, the sounds linked together sound like a /ch/. When a word ends in a /d/ sound, and the following word is either you or your, the sounds linked together sound like a /j/.

   Examples:
   let your = letchur or letchore
   that you = thachu or thatcha
   told you = toldju or toldja

Rule Of Five

It takes from thirty to fifty repetitions to move words and phrases from short term memory to long term memory, but most students (and some teachers) resist this much repetition. The *Rule Of Five* is designed specifically to make the move from short term to long term memory. If you explain that to your students they will understand the process and give less resistance.

1. The teacher repeats the word or phrase *five* times while the student listens.

2. The teacher and student repeat the word or phrase *five* times together.

3. The student repeats the word or phrase *five* times while the teacher listens.

4. The teacher comments and makes corrections as necessary.

5. The student repeats the word or phrase another *five* times.

Always repeat the entire five steps at least once; then repeat additional times if needed. Each time through, the student will say the word or phrase fifteen times, but remember that it takes thirty to fifty repetitions to move the the material into long term memory. You may need to go through the five steps three or four times; use your own judgment and experience as your guide.

A Personal Note

As an International Ministry in a church, we teach English and the Bible in our ESL/Bible classes. A few years ago, the number of students in our International Sunday School was dropping, so we decided to make some changes. We worked out a program that would teach a Christian song along with a Bible verse to the entire group before breaking out into classes. We chose to teach the verse using chanting and we wanted to include a lot of English pronunciation and vocabulary in the process. We also decided to start Sunday School twenty minutes earlier to accommodate the new multi-level *opening assembly* that would be heavy on English and Christian influence. Our goal was that each student would learn the Bible verse in that one session.

Because music is a great way to get rhythm, rate and pronunciation into a student's understanding, we needed a song as part of the program. Since we were teachers and not musicians, we recruited a pianist to improve the music.

Each lesson would focus on a single bible verse or short passage, and we would teach it in many different ways: using *bubbles* to assist in the *rhythm of the language*, using the *chants* to liven up the program, and speaking in *sound units* to improve natural speaking where the words would flow smoothly between breath pauses. We would teach linking rules and practice linking, and sometimes we would add exercises like *fill in the blanks*. And most important, we would do everything many, many times because repetition is the key to remembering.

The changes worked, and the students came back—bringing their friends and family with them.

Each teaching unit in *Section Two* of this book is four pages and represents a complete lesson that we have taught in our program, plus teacher's notes that provide tips and background information. We usually begin by teaching the *words* to a song—one that is simple and English friendly. Some lessons in this book recommend one or two songs, but you can use any ESL friendly song. After teaching the words, we practice getting the *phrases* and *sentences* of the song well rehearsed with lots of repetition. And finally we sing the song several times.

After the song, we move on to the Bible Verse. We read it in sections, with repetition. Often the linking rules and examples are read chorally, and the students begin to learn the rules. Going over the rules every week may seem repetitious to the teacher, but the students need to know why we speak as we do. That helps them transfer the in-class English to the real speaking world. We move on and go over the chant in groups, doing it many times. Repetition is vital. Then, we use other learning strategies found in the section.

And did I mention that *repetition is important?* If you complete a lesson and have a lot of time left over, you have not used enough repetition. First, do the exercise with the whole group then split into two groups. You may even need to work with individuals in some situations. However, when you work with individuals, you must not embarrass them. You should encourage students to speak freely so that their mistakes can be corrected, but you must not allow yourself or the class to laugh at mistakes or make fun of the individual. In other words, you must provide a safe learning environment where students will allow themselves to speak out freely without fear of becoming the object of someone's cruel humor.

In *Section Three*, each lesson is only two pages and the lesson does not contain everything that was in a lesson in section two. You will need to expand it and introduce your own material and teaching methods. Use Section Two as a guide for additional material that may be useful. The material in section three was originally used as a field test to determine the effectiveness of different methods, and many users quickly requested more lessons. Thus, the original book has now expanded.

Finally, *Section Four* is very short and is all about encouraging you to create your own lessons from scratch. You can do it! If you have taught section two, then worked to expand the material in section three, just use that experience and your knowledge as a teacher and you will be surprised at how well your own creations will work. I hope you enjoy using this material and making your own.

Glenda Reece

Section 2

Proverbs 1:5-7

[5]*Let the wise listen and add to their learning, and let the discerning get guidance— for understanding proverbs and parables, the sayings and riddles of the wise. The fear of the Lord is the beginning of knowledge, but fools despise wisdom and discipline.*

Applicable Linking Rules

Be sure to link all words in each sound unit.

Rule #4. When a word ends in a consonant sound and the next word begins with the same consonant sound, the sound is elongated, but never produced twice and no extra filler sound is used.

Examples: *let the, and discipline*

The Rhythm of the Language

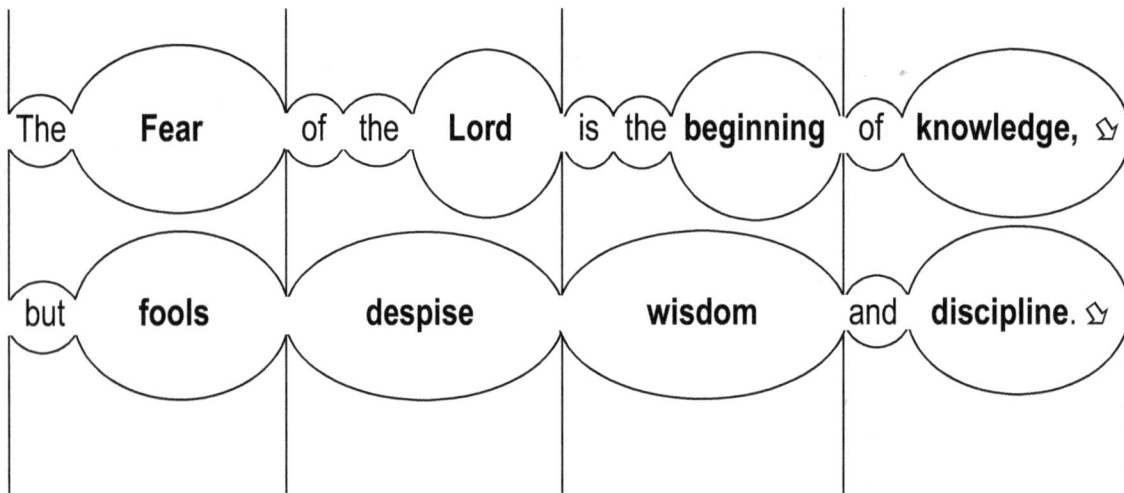

The   Fear   of the **Lord**   is the **beginning** of **knowledge,** ↘

but **fools**   despise   **wisdom**   and **discipline.** ↘

Note: ↘ *is used as a reminder that the voice goes down at the end of sentences and often at the end of sound units.*

Bible Verse Chant

Form two groups. Chant each line and read the verse. Repeat as many times as needed. At first, chant slowly, then speed up to normal speaking rate. Finally, work on English voice quality.

Group 1	Group 2
Let the **wise listen** and **add** to their **learning,**	and let the **discerning** get **guidance—**
for **understanding proverbs** and **parables,**	the **sayings** and **riddles** of the **wise.**
The **fear** of the **Lord** is the **beginning** of **knowledge,**	but **fools despise wisdom** and **discipline.**

Groups 1 & 2

[5]Let the **wise listen** / ☝

and **add** to their **learning,** / ☝

and let the **discerning** get **guidance—** / ☝

for **understanding proverbs** and **parables,** / ☝

the **sayings** and **riddles** / of the **wise.** / ☝

The **fear** of the **Lord** / ☝

is the **beginning** of **knowledge,** / ☝

but **fools despise wisdom** and **discipline.** ☝

Proverbs 1:5-7

Vocabulary and Vocabulary Expansion

Adjective	Noun	Verb	Adverb
Wise	Wisdom		Wisely
Knowledgeable	Knowledge	To know	Knowledgeably
	Guidance Guide	To guide	
Discerning	Discerning	To discern	
	Fear	To fear	
	Saying	To say	
	Learning	To learn	
Despicable		To despise	Despicably

1. Wise: able to make sensible decisions and judgments on the basis of knowledge and experience.

2. Knowledge: general awareness and /or possession of information, facts, ideas, truths or principles.

3. Guidance: advice or counseling; leadership or direction

4. Discerning: showing good judgment and good taste

5. Fear: worry, dread; can be awe or reverence

6. Saying: a proverb or frequently offered information.

7. Learning: knowledge or skill gained through education

8. To despise: to dislike somebody intensely and with contempt.

Teacher Notes

Teaching the proverb should be fun. Start anywhere you like, but I generally begin with the *bubbles* that show the rhythm of the sentences. This visual cue helps students to pick up the rhythm and emphasis of the language.

The *linking rule* explains how to link the words, and improves the rate of speaking, and it helps intermediate and advanced students transfer the classroom exercise into speaking English more clearly. *Vocabulary* and *literary elements* are for the intermediate and advanced students. Do not linger on them or you may discourage the beginners.

The *Fill in the Blank* sections is another means to get repeatition so that students can memorize the verse, and your goal is for them to know the verse by the end of the lesson. Feel free to change which words are omitted. To teach and review, First cover the second verse and teach the first, then switch and teach the second verse while covering the first. Usually, Do these chorally, and have the class put in the blank word from memory. Repeat a few times because repetition is one of the keys to learning.

Fill in the blanks

[5]Let the wise _____ and add to their _____ , and let the discerning get guidance—for understanding _____ and parables, the sayings and riddles of the _____ . The fear of the _____ is the beginning of _____, but fools despise _____ and discipline.

[5]Let the _____ listen and add to their learning, and let the _____ get guidance—for _____ proverbs and parables, the sayings and _____ of the wise. The fear of the Lord is the _____ of knowledge, but _____ despise wisdom and discipline.

Suggested Song

People Need the Lord

When choosing songs for a multi-level group, use good ESL teaching sense. Repetition, simple vocabulary, and a good memorable tune work wonders.

Proverbs 1:20, 33; 2:6

[1:20]*Wisdom calls aloud in the street, she raises her voice in the public squares.*
[1:33]*but whoever listens to me will live in safety and be at ease, without fear of harm.*
[2:6]*For the Lord gives wisdom, and from his mouth come knowledge and understanding.*

Applicable Linking Rules

Be sure to link all words in each sound unit.

Rule #1. Linking with /y/ or /w/ glides commonly occurs when one word or syllable ends in a tense vowel or diphthong and the next word or syllable begins with a vowel.

Example: *Be at* is pronounced *be* [(y)] *at*

Rule #2. When a word ending with a single consonant is followed by a word beginning with a vowel, the consonant is held and it sounds like it belongs to both words.

Examples: *calls aloud, and understanding*

The Rhythm of the Language

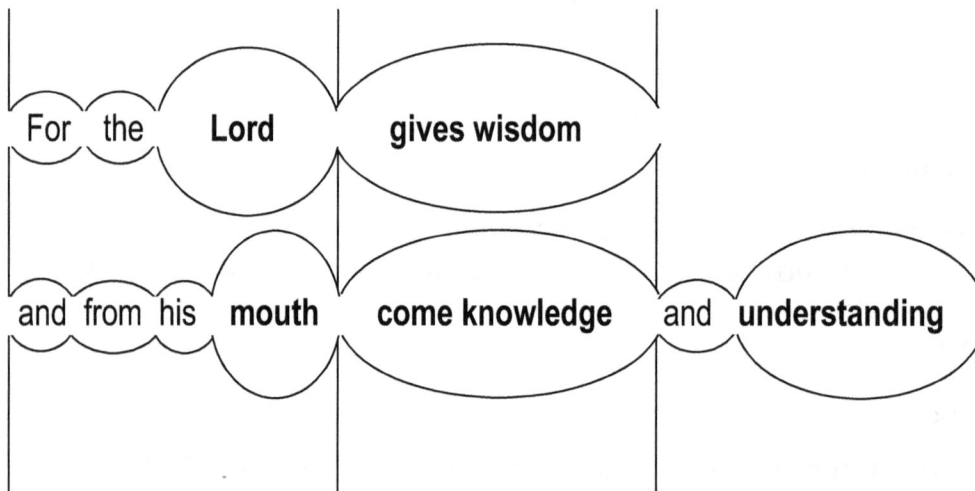

Bible Verse Chant

Form two groups. Chant each line and read the verse. Repeat as many times as needed. At first, chant slowly, then speed up to normal speaking rate. Finally, work on English voice quality.

Group 1	*Group 2*
Wisdom calls aloud in the **street**	She **raises** her **voice** in the **public squares**.
But **whoever listens** to me	**Will live** in **safety** and be at **ease**.
Without **fear** of **harm**.	Without **fear** of **harm**.
For the **Lord** **gives wisdom**	And from his **mouth** **come knowledge** and **understanding**.
For the **Lord** **gives wisdom**	And from his **mouth** **come knowledge** and **understanding**.

Groups 1 & 2

[20]**Wisdom calls aloud** in the **street**, / she **raises** her **voice** / in the **public squares**. / ↘

[33]but **whoever listens** to me / **will live** in **safety** and be at **ease**, / without **fear** of **harm**. / ↘

[6]For the Lord **gives wisdom**, / ↘

and from his **mouth** / **come knowledge** and **understanding**. ↘

Proverbs 1:20, 33 and 2:6

Note: ↘ *is used as a reminder that the voice goes down at the end of sentences and often at the end of sound units*

Literary Elements

Personification

1. Somebody who is an embodiment or perfect example of something

2. A representation of an abstract quality or notion as a human being, especially in art or literature. Wisdom is not a person, but I could say Wisdom gave me insights.

3. The attribution of human qualities to objects or abstract notions. *The sun smiled on me today.*

Encarta® World English Dictionary
© 1999 Microsoft Corporation. All rights reserved.
Developed for Microsoft by Bloomsbury Publishing Plc.

Synonym

A word that means the same, or almost the same, as another word in the same language, either in all of its uses or in a particular context.

Example:
Embodiment: Representation, Characterization, Distillation

Teacher Notes

Not every section of a chant is put into bubbles. Go carefully over the parts that are not. This chant has wisdom personified. Use an example, such as *The sun is smiling today.* Obviously the sun is an object, and the students will realize that personification takes place in every language. Have fun with this concept.

The synonyms listed in the vocabulary section might be really new to the students. It is a good time to use the pronunciation technique called **backward build-up**. Carefully say the word, like *embodiment.* Then say the last two syllables correctly. Do not overstress the vowels, for one or more could be a schwa, the unstressed /ə/ or uh sound. Regional dialects differ here. To continue, repeat 5 times, /də mənt/, then add /bod/, saying /bod di ment/ about 5 times, finally, say em bod di ment. See if all the students can get all four syllables so that it sounds like English. Backward build-up works very well with most three to seven syllable words. And it can be a lot of fun for everyone. Use the rule of five here.

Read everything chorally. The more the learner reads the words and repeats them, the more practice he gets.

Fill in the Blanks

[20]Wisdom calls _____ in the street, she _____ her voice in the public _____. [33]but whoever _____ to me will live in _____ and be at ease, without _____ of harm. [6]For the _____ gives wisdom, and from his _____ come knowledge and _____.

Proverb 1:20, 33; 2:6. Old Testament

[20]Wisdom calls aloud in the _____, she raises her voice in the _____ squares [33]but whoever listens to me will _____ in safety and be at _____, without fear of harm. [6]For the Lord gives _____, and from his mouth come _____ and understanding

Proverb 1:20, 33; 2:6. Old Testament

Suggested Song

Open Our Eyes Lord

Proverbs 3:11-12

[11]*My son, do not despise the Lord's discipline and do not resent his rebuke, because the Lord disciplines those he loves, as a father the son he delights in.*

Applicable Linking Rules

Be sure to link all words in each sound unit.

Rule #4. When a word ends in a consonant sound and the next word begins with the same consonant sound, the sound is elongated, but never produced twice and no extra filler sound is used.

Examples: *not despise, Lord disciplines,*

The Rhythm of the Language

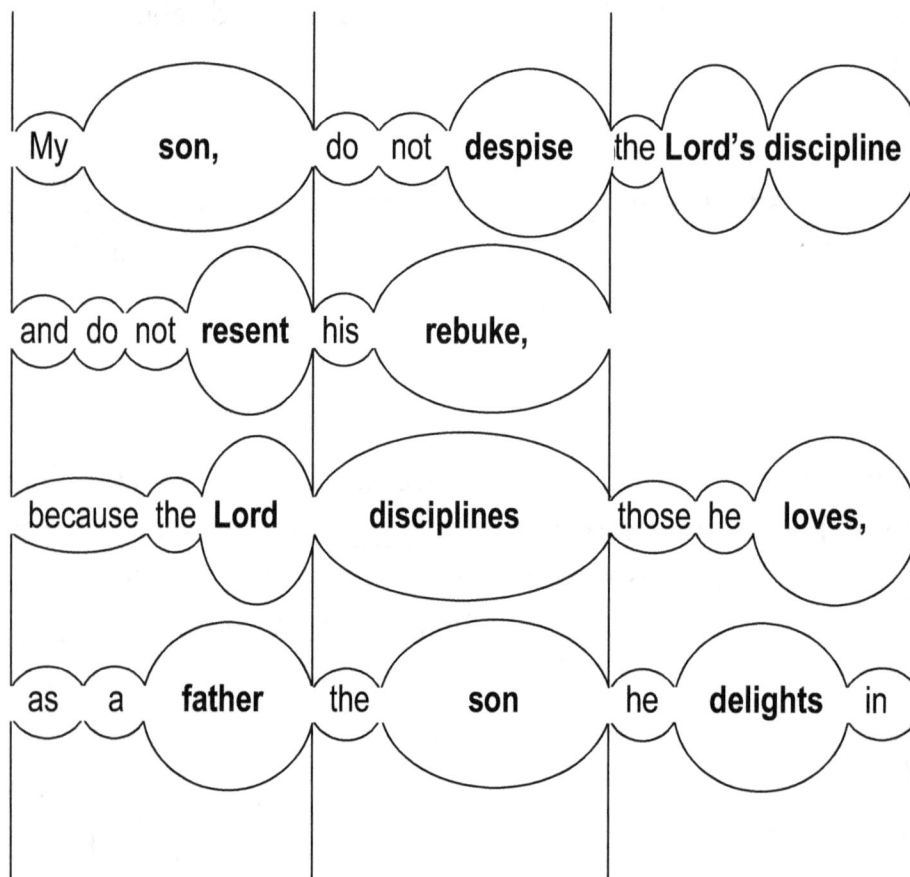

My son, do not despise the Lord's discipline

and do not resent his rebuke,

because the Lord disciplines those he loves,

as a father the son he delights in

Bible Verse Chant

Form two groups. Chant each line and read the verse. Repeat as many times as needed. At first, chant slowly, then speed up to normal speaking rate. Finally, work on English voice quality.

Group 1	*Group 2*
My **son**,	Do not **despise** the **Lord's** discipline
And do not **resent** his **rebuke**,	Because the **Lord disciplines** those he **loves**,
As a **father** the **son**	He **delights** in.
Why not? I resent discipline!	Because the Lord and the father love you.
Discipline is not love!	Discipline helps you grow the right way.
Yes, discipline is love!	Yes, discipline is love!

Groups 1 & 2

[11]My **son**, / ↘

do not **despise** / the **Lord's discipline** / ↘

and do not **resent** / his **rebuke**, / ↘

because the **Lord disciplines** / those he **loves**, / ↘

as a **father** / the **son** / he **delights** in. ↘

Proverbs 3:11-12

Note: ↘ *is used as a reminder that the voice goes down at the end of sentences and often at the end of sound units.*

Vocabulary and Vocabulary Expansion

Adjective	Noun	Verb	Adverb
Despicable		To despise	Despicably
	Discipline	To discipline	
Resentful	Resentment	To resent	Resentfully
	Rebuke	To rebuke	
Delightful		To delight in	Delightfully
	Spanking	To spank	

1. Despise: to dislike somebody or something intensely and with contempt. Hate, look down on.

2. Discipline: the practice of ensuring that people obey rules by teaching them to do so and punishing them if they do not. Order, control, obedience.

3. Resent: to feel upset because of a perceived wrong or injustice. Dislike, be offended by.

4. Rebuke: to criticize or reprimand somebody, usually sharply. Reprimand, "haul over the coals".

5. Delight in: to take great joy or pleasure in. Happiness.

6. Spank: to strike somebody, usually on the buttocks with the open hand in punishment.

Teacher Notes

Occasionally, as in this chant, a comment is added. Here it is in the form of a question and answer. Add a lot of emotion and expression to this. Often people of all ages resent discipline. It does have a purpose. This type of chant can give rise to conversation and discussion about resentment and even discipline.

Word Thermometer
despise hate resent

In vocabulary, a word thermometer could be used here, such as despise, hate, resent. You can always add other words, but *despise* is the top or the "hottest" in this thermometer. You can also add words like *abhor, detest, be offended by,* and *dislike.*

Suggested Song

His Name Is Wonderful

Again, repeat any songs the students have learned. This will help the class recall and new students will get a feeling for the continuation of the class. Try to review each song for three sessions of your class. That way you are putting the tune and the words into long-term memory.

Proverbs 3:27-30

[27]*Do not withhold good from those who deserve it, when it is in your power to act.*
[28] *Do not say to your neighbor, "Come back later; I'll have it tomorrow"— when you now have it with you.* [29] *Do not plot harm against your neighbor, who lives trustfully near you.* [30] *Do not accuse a man for no reason—when he has done you no harm.*

The Rhythm of the Language

Do not withhold **good** from those who **deserve** it

when it is in your **power** to **act.**

Do not say to your **neighbor,** "Come back **later;** I'll give it **tomorrow"**

when you **now** have it **with** you.

Bible Verse Chant

Form two groups. Chant each line and read the verse. Repeat as many times as needed. At first, chant slowly, then speed up to normal speaking rate. Finally, work on English voice quality.

Group 1	*Group 2*

Do not withhold **good**
    from those
    who **deserve** it,
	when it is in your **power**
	    to **act**

Do not say
    to your **neighbor**,
	"Come back **later**;
	    I'll give it **tomorrow**"

When you **now**	have it **with** you.

Do not **plot harm**
    against your **neighbor**,
	Who **lives** trustfully
	    near you.

Do not **accuse** a man
    for no reason—
	When he has done you
	    no harm.

Groups 1 & 2

[27]Do not withhold **good** / from those who **deserve** it, / �
when it is in your **power** / to **act**. / ♻

[28] Do not say to your **neighbor**, / ♻
"Come back **later**; / I'll have it **tomorrow**"— / ♻
when you **now** / have it **with** you. / ♻

[29] Do not **plot harm** / against your **neighbor**, / ♻
who **lives** trustfully near you. / [30] ♻

Do not **accuse** a man / for no reason— / ♻
when he has done you / no harm. / ♻

Proverbs 3:27-30

Vocabulary and Vocabulary Expansion

Admonition

1. a mild but earnest rebuke

2. advice for or against doing something

Synonyms

Caution, Warning

Reprimand, Rebuke

Reproach, Scolding

Antonym

Approval

Encarta® World English Dictionary
© 1999 Microsoft Corporation. All rights reserved.
Developed for Microsoft by Bloomsbury Publishing Plc.

Teacher Notes

Fill in the blanks exercises help the students with memory. A cloze test exercise deletes every 6th or 7th word and checks the student for the correct flow of the language. Here the blanks take out selected words the first time, and other words the second time, so this is not really a cloze test. The more you manipulate and repeat the verses the clearer the understanding will become. Write this on the board, on a separate piece of paper to take home or however you choose to do it. Perhaps it would make good homework.

Not every teacher suggestion can be done in every class, but varied teaching tricks and techniques help the students stay interested and learn.

Open Our Eyes Lord is a good example of an ESL beginner song. It is easy to insert motions and do TPR (Total Physical Response). For example, open and close your eyes, reach out with your hands, touch someone, cup your hands behind your ears for listen. Review any songs taught previously.

Fill in the Blanks

[27]Do not withhold _____ from those who deserve it, when it is in your _____ to act. [28] Do not _____ to your neighbor, "Come back later; I'll have it _____ "— when you now have it with you. [29] Do not _____ harm against your neighbor, who lives _____ near you. [30] Do not accuse a man for no _____ —when he has done you _____ harm.

[27]Do not _____ good from those who _____ it, when it is in your power to act. [28] Do not say to your _____ , "Come back _____ ; I'll have it tomorrow"— when you now have it with you. [29] Do not plot _____ against your neighbor, who lives trustfully near _____ . [30] Do not _____ a man for no reason—when he has done you no harm.

Suggested Songs

Come, Now Is The Time To Worship
Open Our Eyes Lord.

Proverbs 4:23-27

²³*Above all else, guard your heart, for it is the wellspring of life.* ²⁴ *Put away perversity from your mouth; keep corrupt talk away from your lips.* ²⁵*Let your eyes look straight ahead, fix your gaze directly before you.* ²⁶*Make level paths for your feet and take only ways that are firm.* ²⁷*Do not swerve to the right or to the left; keep your foot from evil.*

The Rhythm of the Language

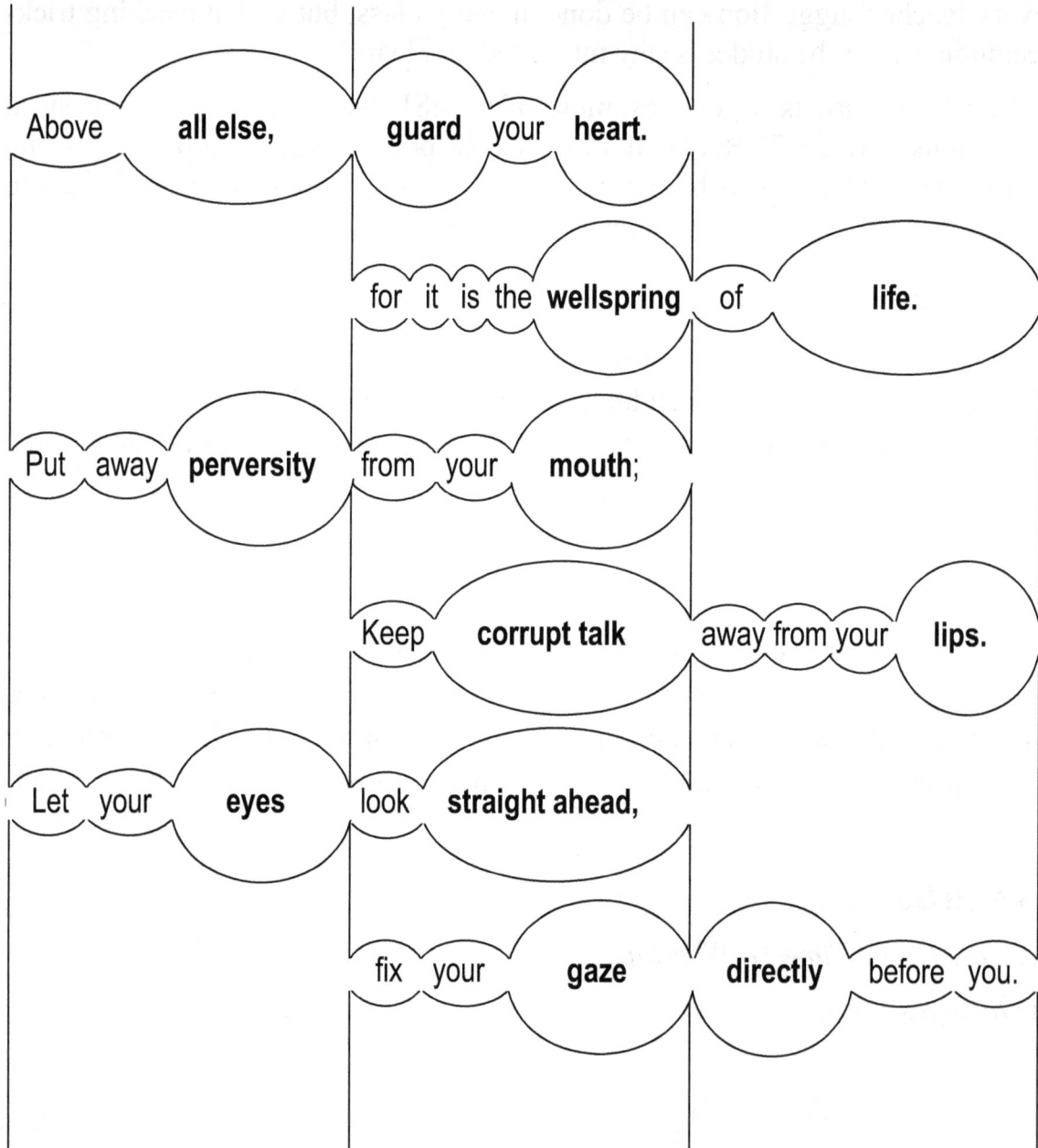

Above **all else,** **guard** your **heart.**

for it is the **wellspring** of **life.**

Put away **perversity** from your **mouth;**

Keep **corrupt talk** away from your **lips.**

Let your **eyes** look **straight ahead,**

fix your **gaze** **directly** before you.

Bible Verse Chant

Form two groups. Chant each line and read the verse. Repeat as many times as needed. At first, chant slowly, then speed up to normal speaking rate. Finally, work on English voice quality.

Group 1	**_Group 2_**
Above **all else**,	**guard** your **heart**,
for it is the **wellspring**	of **life**.

Groups 1 & 2
[23]Above **all else**, / **guard** your **heart**, / ↘ for it is the **wellspring** / of **life**. / ↘ [24] Put away **perversity** / from **your** mouth; / ↘ keep **corrupt talk** / away from your **lips**. / ↘ [25]Let your **eyes** / look **straight ahead**, / ↘ fix your **gaze** / **directly** before you. / ↘ [26]Make level **paths** for your **feet** / ↘ and **take** only **ways** / that are **firm**. / ↘ [27]Do not **swerve** to the **right** / or to the **left**; / ↘ keep your **foot** from evil. ↘

Group 1	**_Group 2_**
Above all **else**,	**guard** your **heart**,
for it is the **wellspring**	of **life**.

Note: ↘ *is used as a reminder that the voice goes down at the end of sentences and often at the end of sound units.*

Vocabulary and Vocabulary Expansion

Adjective	Noun	Verb	Adverb
	Wellspring		
	Guardian	To guard	Guardedly
Perverse	Perversity		Perversely
Corrupt	Corruption	To corrupt	
	Gaze	To gaze	
		To swerve	

1. Wellspring: a source of a spring or stream of water; a plentiful source or supply of something.

2. Guard: to protect or watch over; sentinel.

3. Guardian: one who protects.

4. Perversity: to be unreasonable or willfully persisting in doing wrong.

5. Corrupt: immoral or dishonest; to introduce intentional errors.

6. Gaze: to fix your eyes on, stare, look.

7. Swerve: to make a sudden change in direction

Teacher Notes

The vocabulary in this chant is extensive and of high intermediate or advanced level. Spend more time on this, if possible. Beginners can use it as pronunciation practice.

The Flap /d/ Rule

In North American English, the /t/ sound takes on a unique quality after either a vowel, an /r/, or an unstressed syllable. The tongue touches the tooth ridge very briefly, like a flap or a tap, and it is voiced. This sounds the same as when /d/ is found. There is little or no sound difference in words like *catty* and *caddy*. These flaps also occur in sentences and across word boundaries. *Part it on the side* sounds like *pardit on the side*. The Flap /d/ is found only in North American English.

In this verse, it is found in *Put away perversity*.

Fill in the Blanks

²³Above all else, _____ your heart, for it is the wellspring of _____. ²⁴ Put away perversity from your _____; keep corrupt _____ away from your lips. ²⁵Let your _____ look straight ahead, fix your _____ directly before you. ²⁶Make level _____ for your feet and take only ways that are _____. ²⁷Do not swerve to the _____ or to the left; keep your foot from _____.

²³_____ all else, guard your _____, for it is the _____ of life. ²⁴ Put away perversity _____ your mouth; keep _____ talk away from your lips. ²⁵Let your eyes _____ straight ahead, fix your gaze _____ before you. ²⁶Make_____ paths for your feet and take only _____ that are firm. ²⁷Do not _____ to the right or to the left; keep your foot from evil.

Suggested Song

Great Is Thy Faithfulness

Proverbs 6:6-8

[6] *Go to the ant, you sluggard; consider its ways and be wise!*

[7] *It has no commander, no overseer or ruler,*

[8] *yet it stores its provisions in summer and gathers its food at harvest.*

The Rhythm of the Language

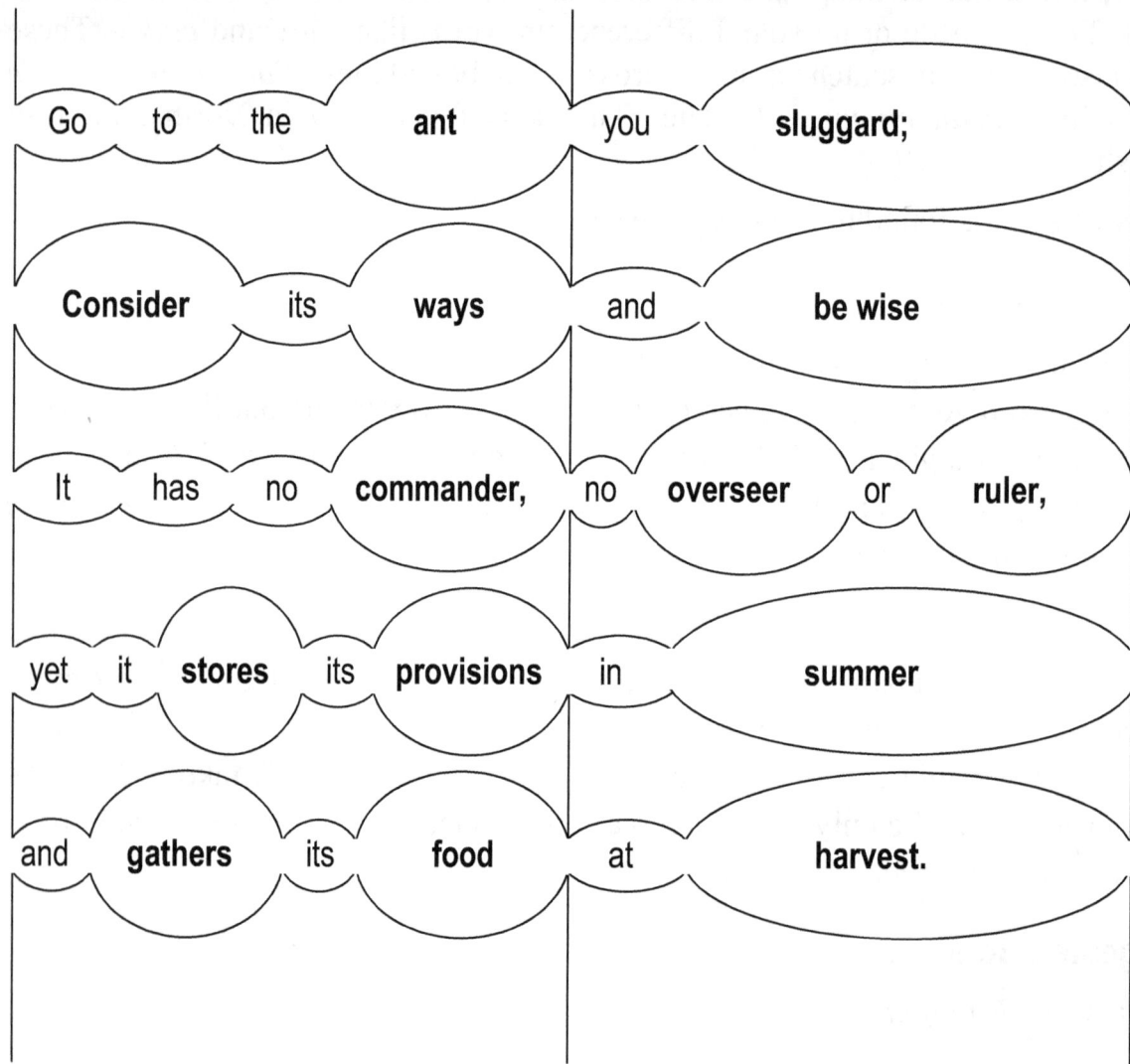

Go to the ant you **sluggard;**

Consider its **ways** and **be wise**

It has no **commander,** no **overseer** or **ruler,**

yet it **stores** its **provisions** in **summer**

and **gathers** its **food** at **harvest.**

Bible Verse Chant

Form two groups. Chant each line and read the verse. Repeat as many times as needed. At first, chant slowly, then speed up to normal speaking rate. Finally, work on English voice quality.

Group 1	Group 2
Go to the **ant**, you **sluggard**,	**consider** its **ways** and be **wise**!
It has no **commander**,	no **overseer** or **ruler**,
yet it **stores** its **provisions** in **summer**	and **gathers** its **food** at **harvest**.

Groups 1 & 2

[6]Go to the **ant**, / you **sluggard**; / **consider** its ways / and be **wise**! ↘

[7] It has no **commander**, / no **overseer** or **ruler**, / ↘

[8]yet it **stores** its **provisions** / in **summer** / and **gathers** its **food** / at **harvest**. ↘

Note: ↘ *is used as a reminder that the voice goes down at the end of sentences and often at the end of sound units.*

Vocabulary and Vocabulary Expansion

1. Admonition: A mild rebuke; advice about doing something either for it or against it.

2. Sluggard: Someone who avoids word or physical exertion. Sluggishly lazy.

3. Ways: Actions, behavior

4. Commander: Military officer

5. Ruler: Monarch, leader, head of state

6. Overseer: Supervisor, boss

7. Provisions: Food and supplies

8. To gather: To pick or harvest a crop

9. Harvest: The season when crops are gathered

Encarta® World English Dictionary
© 1999 Microsoft Corporation. All rights reserved.
Developed for Microsoft by Bloomsbury Publishing Plc.

Teacher Notes

This chant is part one of two, Proverbs 6:6-8 and Proverbs 6:9-11.

Since many of the proverbs are actually admonitions, I decided to actually teach the word. A multi-level class can handle some larger words, and I chose this even though it is not in the chant or verse itself. Advice, especially a warning, is an admonition.

The vocabulary is fun to teach, especially the word *sluggard*.

Always work on the correct and comfortable pronunciation of the content words. This will take some use of backward buildup and syllable work.

Power English can be taught here because these sentences are commands. Make sure the students say this with power and authority. Remember Jesus taught with authority.

Fill in the Blanks

[6]Go to the ant, you _____; consider its ways and be wise!

[7] It has no _____, no overseer or ruler,

[8] yet it stores its provisions in _____and gathers its _____ at harvest.

[6]Go to the _____, you sluggard; _____ its ways and be _____!

[7] It has no commander, no overseer or _____,

[8] yet it _____ its provisions in summer and gathers its food at _____.

Suggested Songs

In Christ There Is No East or West

Doxology

Proverbs 6:9-11

[9]*How long will you lie there, you sluggard? When will you get up from your sleep?*

[10]*A little sleep, a little slumber, a little folding of the hands to rest-*

[11]*And poverty will come on you like a bandit and scarcity like an armed man.*

The Rhythm of the Language

How long will you **lie there** you **sluggard?**

When will you **get up** from your **sleep?**

A little **sleep,** a little **slumber,**

a little **folding** of the **hands** to **rest—**

and **poverty** will **come on** you like a **bandit**

and **scarcity** like an **armed man.**

Bible Verse Chant

Form two groups. Chant each line and read the verse. Repeat as many times as needed. At first, chant slowly, then speed up to normal speaking rate. Finally, work on English voice quality.

Group 1	*Group 2*
How long will you **lie there**, you **sluggard**?	When will you **get up** from your **sleep**?
A little **sleep**, a little **slumber**, a little **folding** of the **hands** to **rest**—	And **poverty** will **come on** you like a **bandit** and **scarcity** like an **armed man**.

Groups 1 & 2

[6]Go to the **ant**, / you **sluggard**; / **consider** its **ways** / and be **wise**! /

[7]It has no **commander**, / no **overseer** or **ruler**, /

[8]yet it **stores** its **provisions** / in **summer** / and **gathers** its **food** / at **harvest**. /

[9]How long will you **lie there**, / you **sluggard**? / When will you **get up** / from your **sleep**? /

[10]A little **sleep**, / a little **slumber**, / a little **folding** of the **hands** / to **rest**— /

[11]And **poverty** / will **come on** you / like a **bandit** / and **scarcity** / like an **armed man**. /

Proverbs 6:6-11

Synonyms and Vocabulary Expansion

1. Sleep: Slumber, rest, nap, doze, siesta, forty winks, catnap

2. Poverty: Not having enough money to take care of basic needs such as food, clothing and housing.

3. Scarcity: An insufficient supply of something. Lack of, insufficiency, scarceness

Antonym or opposite

Scaricity: abundance, plenty.

Teacher Notes

This continuation of the proverb from the previous lesson completes the admonition. Continue to work for power English and help the students say the words confidently. Here you are looking for confidence, not volume. Have the class say the words strongly, but softly. That is also great use of power English.

Fill in the blanks

[9]How _____ will you lie there, you _____? When will you _____ up from your sleep?

[10]A little _____, a little slumber, a little _____ of the hands to rest—

[11]And poverty will _____ on you like a bandit and _____ like an armed man.

[9]How long will you _____ there, you sluggard? When will you get up from your _____?

[10]A _____ sleep, a little slumber, a little folding of the _____ to rest—

[11]And _____ will come on you like a bandit and scarcity like an _____ man.

Suggested Songs

Deep and Wide

Lonesome Valley

Try doing some Total Physical Response (TPR) with *Deep and Wide.* The hand motions illustrate the meaning quite well.

Proverbs 9:7-8

[7]*Whoever corrects a mocker invites insult; whoever rebukes a wicked man incurs abuse.*

[8]*Do not rebuke a mocker or he will hate you; rebuke a wise man and he will love you.*

Applicable Linking Rules

Rule #1. Linking with /y/ or /w/ glides commonly occurs when one word or syllable ends in a tense vowel or diphthong and the next word or syllable begins with a vowel.

Example: *who*ever = *who* [(w)]*ever*

The Rhythm of the Language

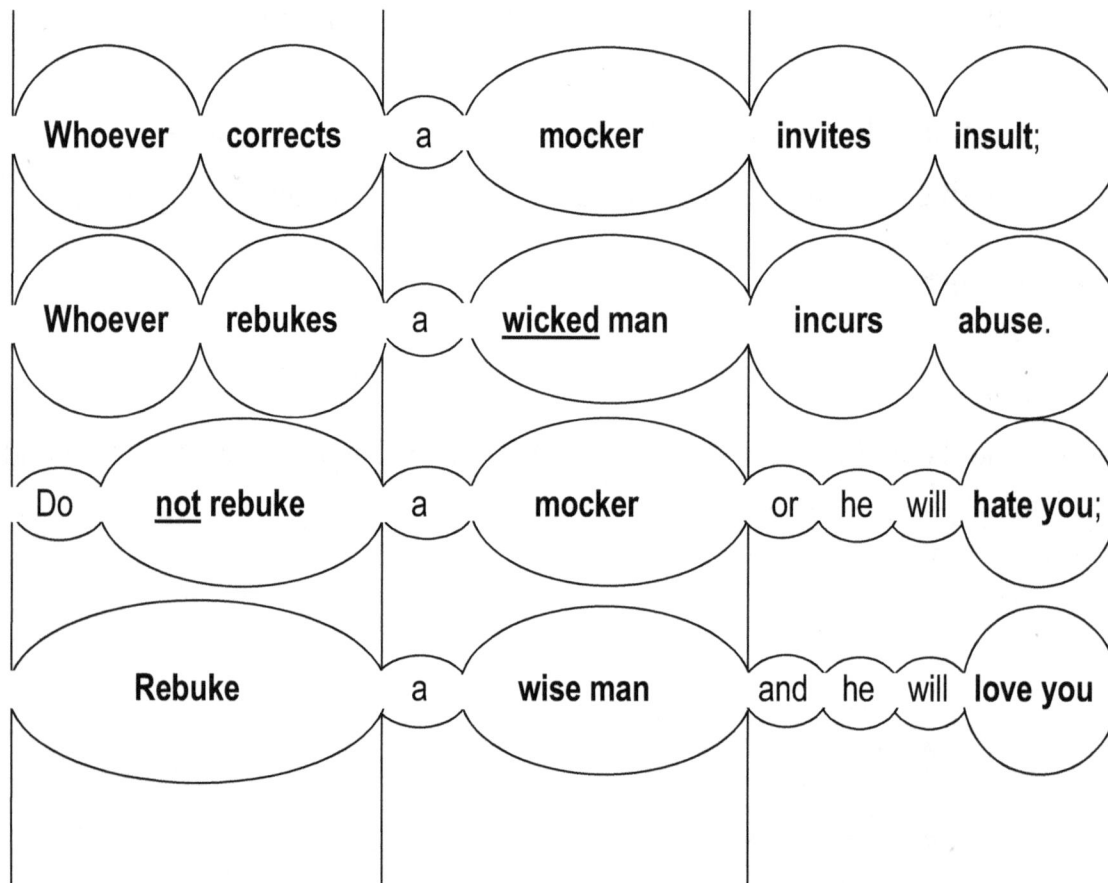

Whoever   corrects   a   mocker   invites   insult;

Whoever   rebukes   a   <u>wicked</u> man   incurs   abuse.

Do   **<u>not</u> rebuke**   a   mocker   or   he   will   **hate you;**

Rebuke   a   wise man   and   he   will   **love you**

Bible Verse Chant

Form two groups. Chant each line and read the verse. Repeat as many times as needed. At first, chant slowly, then speed up to normal speaking rate. Finally, work on English voice quality.

Group 1	*Group 2*
Whoever corrects a **mocker**	**Invites insult;**
Whoever rebukes a <u>**wicked**</u> **man**	**Incurs abuse.**
Do <u>**not**</u> **rebuke** a **mocker**	Or he will **hate you**.
Rebuke a **wise man**	And he will **love you**.

Groups 1 & 2

[7] **Whoever corrects** / a **mocker** / **invites insult**; / ↘
whoever rebukes / a **wicked man** / **incurs abuse**. / ↘

[8] Do **not rebuke** / a **mocker** / or he will **hate you**; / ↘
rebuke / a **wise man** / and he will **love you**. / ↘

[9]**Instruct** a **wise man** / and he will be **wiser still**; / ↘
teach a **righteous man** / and he will **add** to his **learning**. ↘

Proverbs 9:7-9

Note: ↘ *is used as a reminder that the voice goes down at the end of sentences and often at the end of sound units.*

Synonyms and Vocabulary Expansion

1. Advice: Recommendation, counsel, guidance, admonition (admonition is advice that is a warning.)

2. Mocker: scorner, scoffer; one who ridicules another.

3. Wicked: (adj.) evil, depraved, immoral, wrong.

4. To Rebuke: criticize, reprimand, scold

5. Insult: Offense, rudeness, verbal abuses, slight

6. To Teach: Instruct

7. Abuse: Mistreatment, insult, neglect, cruelty

8. To incur: Experience unpleasantness, invite

Opposite Pairs

Mocker	Supporter
Insult	Compliment
Hate	Love
Rebuke	Praise
Abuse	Kindness
Incur	Avoid

Teacher Notes

Review is really important in the learning process. Always try to review a verse or a song at least three times. It is a fun day to sing the songs they have learned and to go over several of the verses.

Again, vocabulary is important here. Most students in a multi-level class do not know all these words. High beginner to advanced students take this verse very seriously.

Fill in the Blanks

Whoever _____ a mocker _____ insult; whoever rebukes a _____ man incurs abuse.

[8] Do not _____ a mocker or he will _____ you; rebuke a _____ man and he will love you.

[9]Instruct a wise _____ and he will _____ wiser still; teach a _____ man and he will add to _____ learning.

_____ corrects a mocker invites _____; whoever rebukes a wicked man _____ abuse.

[8] Do _____ rebuke a mocker or _____ will hate you; _____ a wise man and he will _____ you.

_____ a wise man and he _____ _____ wiser still; teach a _____ man and he will add to his _____.

Suggested Songs

He Lives

Lonesome Valley

Proverbs 15:1 & 4

[1]A gentle answer turns away wrath, but a harsh word stirs up anger.

[4]The tongue that brings healing is a tree of life, but a deceitful tongue crushes the spirit.

Applicable Linking Rules

Rule #2. When a word ending with a single consonant is followed by a word beginning with a vowel, the consonant is held and it sounds like it belongs to both words.

Turns away, stirs up, But a, is a

The Rhythm of the Language

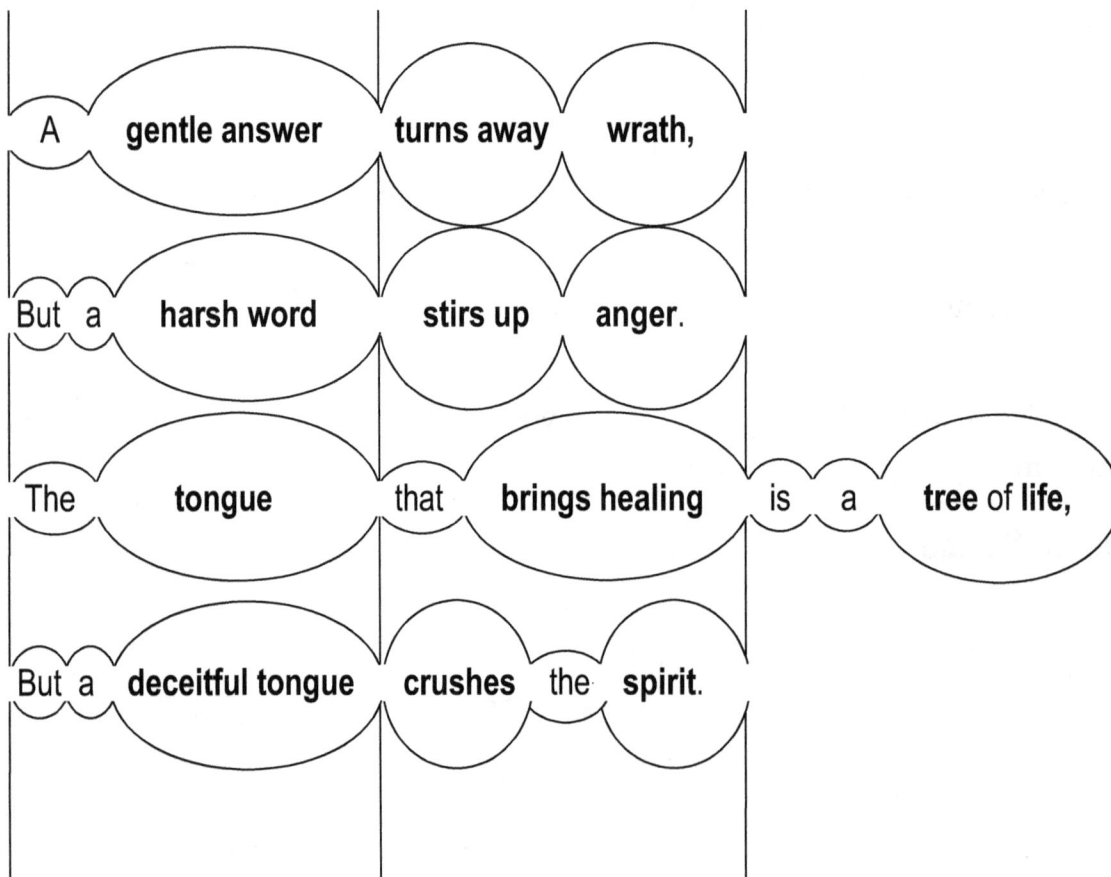

Bible Verse Chant

Form two groups. Chant each line and read the verse. Repeat as many times as needed. At first, chant slowly, then speed up to normal speaking rate. Finally, work on English voice quality.

Group 1	*Group 2*
A **gentle answer** turns away wrath,	but a **harsh word** stirs up anger.
The **tongue** that **brings healing**	is a **tree** of **life**,
but a **deceitful tongue** crushes the **spirit**.	but a **deceitful tongue** crushes the **spirit**.

Groups 1 & 2
[1]A **gentle answer** / turns away wrath, / but a **harsh word** / stirs up anger. /   [4]The **tongue** / that **brings healing** / is a **tree** of **life**, /   but a **deceitful tongue** / crushes the **spirit**.   Proverbs 15:1 and 4

Vocabulary and Vocabulary Expansion

1. Gentle: Having a mild or kind nature. Calm; kind; tender; moderate

2. Wrath: Anger and fury often marked by a desire for revenge. Anger; rage; fury.

3. Harsh: Cruel; severe; insensitive; unsympathetic.

4. Anger: A feeling of extreme annoyance. Fury; rage.

5. Tongue: The words or speech

6. Deceitful: Dishonest; deceiving; untrustworthy.

7. Crush: To humiliate; to devastate; to squash.

Teacher Notes

Use the vocabulary, expansion words or synonyms as a chance to practice pronunciation. Many of the words on the Vocabulary page have a schwa sound in them.

Gentle Gen təl	Moderate mo der ət	Cruel cru əl	Severe sə vere
Unsympathetic un sym pə the tic	Annoyance ə noy ənce	Devastate de və state.	Insensitive in sen sə tive

Work with the schwa—the unstressed vowel is the most used single sound in English. Most international speakers of English are unaware of it, and therefore are frequently misunderstood, or are self-conscious about their speech, but don't know what is missing. The phonetic symbol for the schwa is /ə/. Remember the *stressed* sound that is almost identical to the unstressed schwa is the sound found in the word *up*.

Choral reading is a good technique in any level of ESL. You can read in sound units and have the class repeat. You want them to sound like you so tell them, "Make my voice. Sound like me." Voice Quality English can be taught from the beginning if the teacher insists the language sound like normal English

Fill in the Blanks

[1]A gentle _____ turns away wrath, but a _____ word stirs up anger.

[4]The tongue that brings _____ is a tree of _____, but a deceitful _____ crushes the spirit.

[1]A gentle answer _____ _____ wrath, but a harsh word stirs up _____.

[4]The _____ that brings healing is a _____ of life, but a deceitful tongue _____ the _____.

Suggested Song

Come, Now Is the Time To Worship

Proverbs 15:27-28

[27]*A greedy man brings trouble to his family, but he who hates bribes will live.*

[28]*The heart of the righteous weighs its answers, but the mouth of the wicked gushes evil.*

Single Sound Pronunciation: Long E

Use a rubber band, and stretch it out to illustrate the long e sound. Many internationals, like Chinese and Spanish, have a very hard time holding this sound long enough. Exaggeration helps here. *Greedy, he, evil.*

The Rhythm of the Language

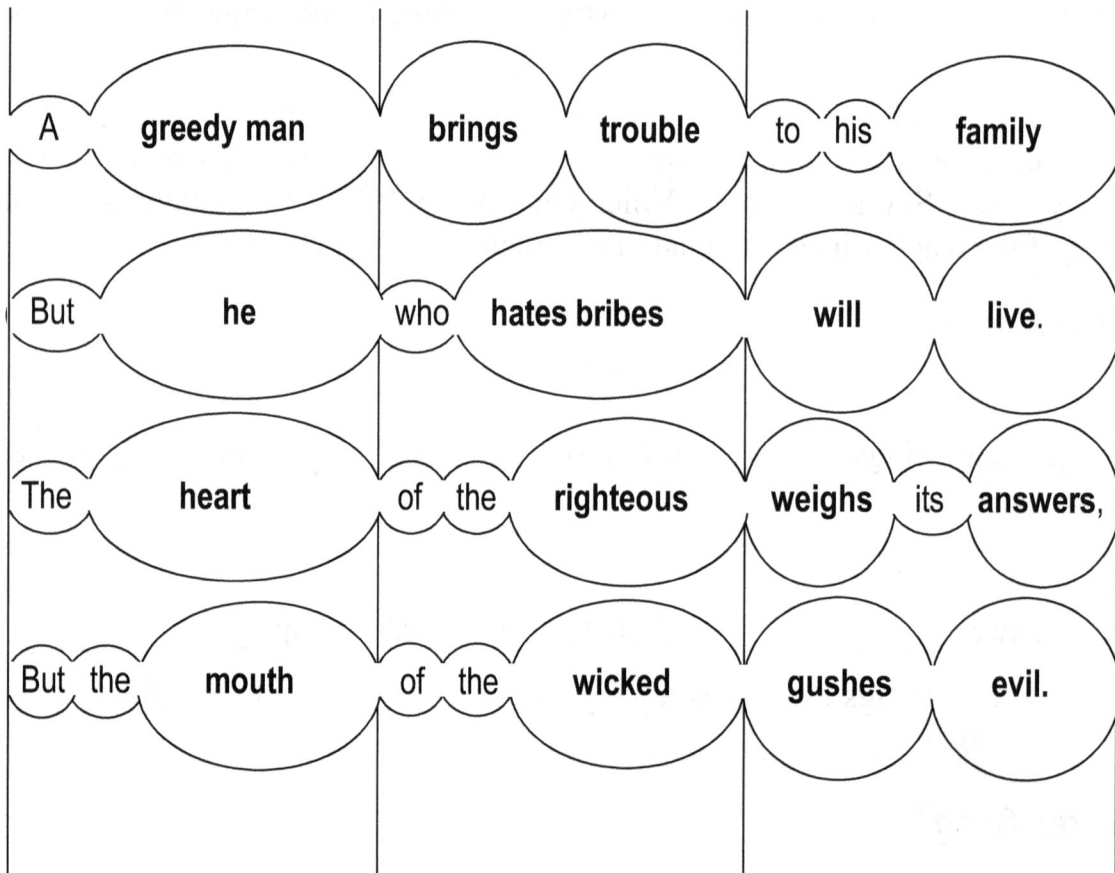

A   greedy man   brings   trouble   to his   family

But   he   who   hates bribes   will   live.

The   heart   of the   righteous   weighs   its   answers,

But the   mouth   of the   wicked   gushes   evil.

Bible Verse Chant

Form two groups. Chant each line and read the verse. Repeat as many times as needed. At first, chant slowly, then speed up to normal speaking rate. Finally, work on English voice quality.

Group 1	*Group 2*

A **greedy man**
    brings trouble
 to his **family**,
	but **he**
	    who **hates bribes**
	 will **live**.

The **heart**
    of the **righteous**
    weighs its **answers**,
	but the **mouth**
	    of the **wicked**
	    gushes evil.

Groups 1 & 2

[27]A **greedy man** / **brings trouble** / to his **family**, ↘ but **he** / who **hates bribes** / will **live**. ↘

[28]The **heart** / of the **righteous** / **weighs** its **answers**, ↘ but the **mouth** / of the **wicked** / **gushes evil**. ↘

Proverbs 15:27-28

Note: ↘ *is used as a reminder that the voice goes down at the end of sentences and often at the end of sound units.*

Vocabulary and Vocabulary Expansion

1. Greedy (adj.), greed (n.): Wanting more or much more than is actually needed.

2. Bribe: money or other items or incentive that is given to persuade somebody to do something, especially something illegal or dishonest. A kickback.

3. To weigh (v.): Here it means to consider or evaluate something. To ponder, evaluate, think about.

4. To gush: (v.) to flow out, or to send a liquid out, rapidly and in large quantities; to speak or behave in an extremely or exaggeratedly enthusiastic, affectionate, or sentimental way

5. Heart: Considered in humans to be the source where the deepest and best feelings are located, and where an individual feels most pain.

Encarta® World English Dictionary
© 1999 Microsoft Corporation. All rights reserved.
Developed for Microsoft by Bloomsbury Publishing Plc.

Opposites

Righteous   Wicked
Good   Bad
Greedy   Moderate

Teacher Notes

Continue working on voice quality English. Shorter verses make it easier to do in class. As a native English speaker, model the English well. Use power English or teach with authority.

Also, chorally read the pronunciation or other rules. Even if students don't truly comprehend, they can mimic and repeat the sounds. Remember, it is an English class as well as a Bible class. Make sure they get a good foundation in oral English.

Fill in the Blanks

[27]A _____ man brings trouble to his _____, but he who _____ bribes will live.

[28]The heart of the _____ weighs its answers, but the _____ of the wicked _____ evil.

[27]A greedy man _____ trouble to his family, but _____ who hates _____ will live.

[28]The _____ of the righteous weighs its _____, but the mouth of the wicked gushes evil.

Suggested Song

People Need the Lord

Proverbs 16:7 and 18

[7]*Commit to the Lord whatever you do, and your plans will succeed.*

[18]*Pride goes before destruction, the haughty spirit before a fall.*

Applicable Linking Rules

Rule #5. The stops in English are t, d, p, k, g, and j. When a stop consonant at the end of one word is followed by a stop consonant at the beginning of the next word, the first stop is not released and that helps the linking. The tongue is in position but before the air is released the next sound is formed.

Example: *Pride goes*

The Rhythm of the Language

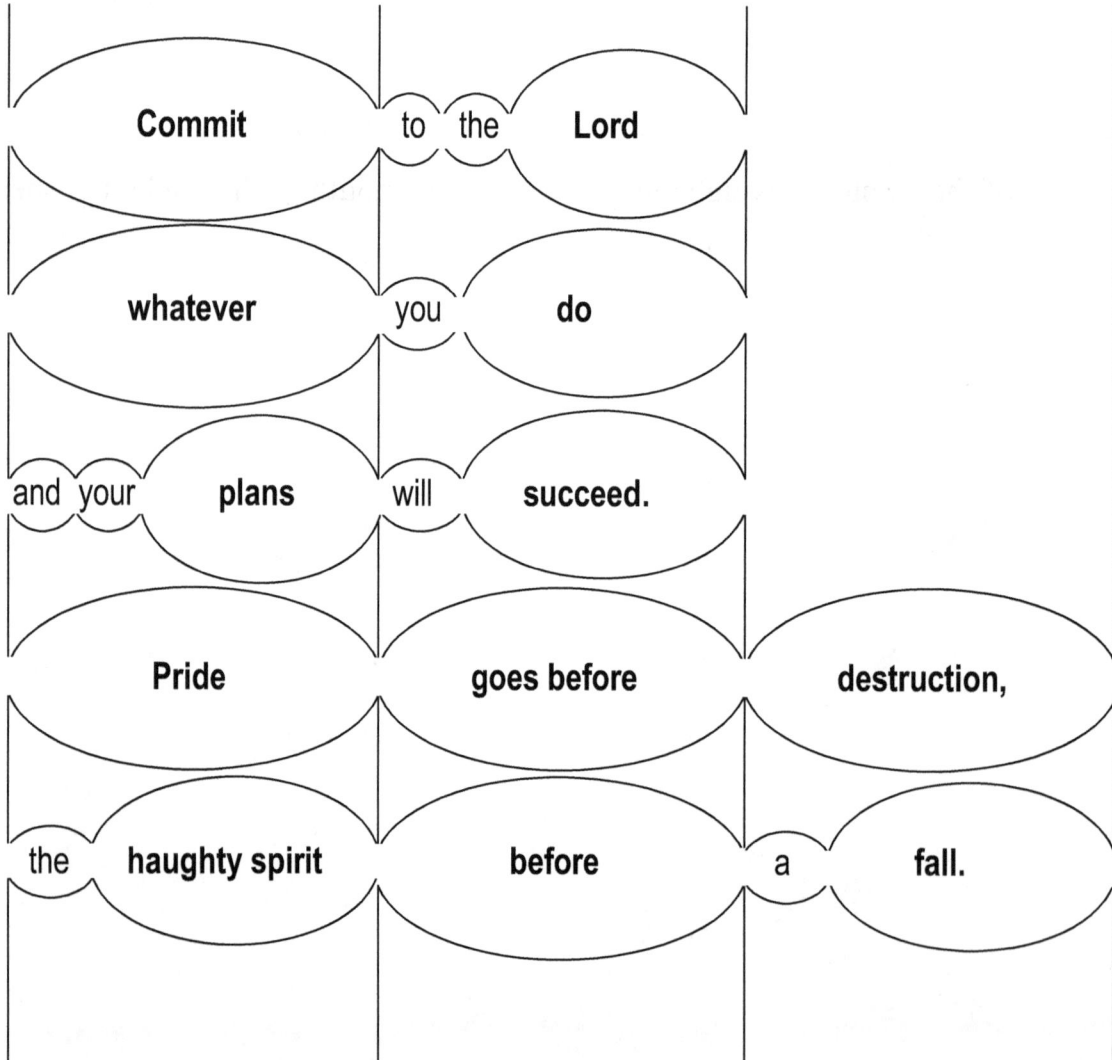

Commit   to the   Lord

whatever   you   do

and your   plans   will   succeed.

Pride   goes before   destruction,

the   haughty spirit   before   a   fall.

Bible Verse Chant

Form two groups. Chant each line and read the verse. Repeat as many times as needed. At first, chant slowly, then speed up to normal speaking rate. Finally, work on English voice quality.

Group 1	*Group 2*
Commit to the **Lord** whatever you **do,**	and your **plans** will **succeed.**
Pride goes before destruction,	the **haughty spirit** before a **fall.**

<table>
<tr><td colspan="2" align="center">Groups 1 & 2</td></tr>
<tr><td colspan="2">⁷Commit to the Lord / whatever you do, / and your plans will succeed. /

¹⁸Pride goes before destruction, / the haughty spirit / before a fall.</td></tr>
</table>

Proverbs 16:7 and 18

Vocabulary and Related Words

Adjective	Noun	Verb	Adverb
	Commitment	To commit	
Successful		To succeed	Successfully
	Plans	To plan	
Proud	Pride		
	Destruction	To destroy	
Haughty			Haughtily

1. Commit (v.) Here it is used as a pledge of devotion or dedication. (This word has many meanings) *We commit ourselves to a good marriage.*

2. Succeed: to achieve something, to thrive. *Can he succeed in his new business?*

3. Plan: Meaning to work out the details carefully. *To be successful, you must plan carefully.*

4. Pride: A haughty attitude, often unjustifiable, that you are better than others. *Successful politicians often develop too much pride and become haughty.*

5. Haughty: behaving in a superior, condescending or arrogant way.

Encarta® World English Dictionary
© 1999 Microsoft Corporation. All rights reserved.
Developed for Microsoft by Bloomsbury Publishing Plc.

Teacher Notes

Marking sound units is certainly not an exact science. Read the passage aloud in a normal tone of voice, keeping the international in mind. If you read very quickly and skip breath pauses, slow down a little and mark the sentence or passage as well as you can. When you teach it, you probably will slow down somewhat.

My sound unit marks may disagree with yours and that is fine. You can re-mark them as you see fit. Practice helps here. Be sure never to break apart a short prepositional phrase or a verb phrase.

If you are just beginning to develop this skill, say the *Pledge of Allegiance* aloud as if with a group. You will hear the natural breaks, and that should help you. English is spoken in sound units or breath units. Most Internationals have never heard of sound units or linking.

Fill in the Blanks

[7]Commit to the _____ whatever you do, and your _____ will succeed.

[18] _____ goes before destruction, the haughty _____ before a fall.

[7]Commit to the Lord _____ you do, and your plans will _____.

[18]Pride _____ before destruction, the _____ spirit before a fall.

Suggested Song

Amazing Grace

Proverbs 16:23-24

[23]*A wise man's heart guides his mouth, and his lips promote instruction.*

[24]*Pleasant words are a honeycomb, sweet to the soul and healing to the bones.*

Applicable Linking Rules

Rule #4. When a word ends in a consonant sound and the next word begins with the same consonant sound, the sound is elongated, but never produced twice and no extra filler sound is used.

Example: *sweet to the soul*

The Rhythm of the Language

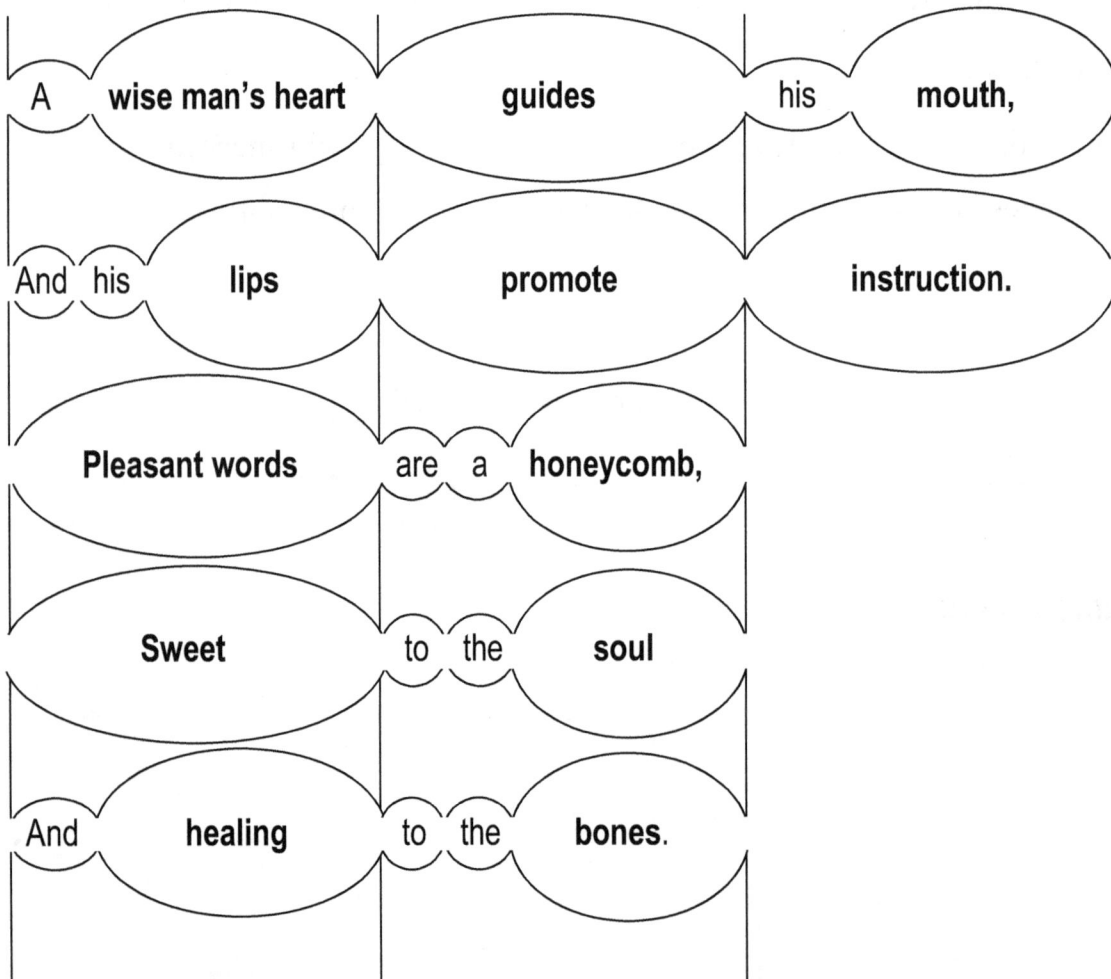

A   wise man's heart   guides   his   mouth,

And his   lips   promote   instruction.

Pleasant words   are a   honeycomb,

Sweet   to the   soul

And   healing   to the   bones.

Bible Verse Chant

Form two groups. Chant each line and read the verse. Repeat as many times as needed. At first, chant slowly, then speed up to normal speaking rate. Finally, work on English voice quality.

<u>**Group 1**</u>	<u>**Group 2**</u>
A **wise man's heart guides** his **mouth**,	and his **lips promote instruction**.
Pleasant words are a **honeycomb**,	**sweet** to the **soul** and **healing** to the **bones**.

<u>***Groups 1 & 2***</u>

[23] A **wise man's heart guides** his **mouth**, / ↘
and his **lips promote instruction**. ↘

[24] **Pleasant words** are a **honeycomb**, / ↘
sweet to the **soul** and **healing** to the **bones**. ↘

Proverbs 16:23-24

Note: ↘ is used as a reminder that the voice goes down at the end of sentences and often at the end of sound units.

Vocabulary and Related Words

Adjective	Noun	Verb	Adverb
	Promotion	To promote	
Pleasant			Pleasantly
Wise	Wisdom		Wisely
	Guide Guidance	To guide	

1. Promote (v.) Here it means to encourage growth and development of something. (This word has many meanings)

2. Pleasant: enjoyable, easy to be around.

3. Heart: Considered in humans to be the source where the deepest and best feelings are located, and where an individual feels most pain.

Teacher Notes

The ...*tion* rule. If a noun ends in ...*tion* or ...*sion*, the sound before it is stressed. It is easy to teach with a rubber band. Just pull the rubber band on the stressed syllable and hold the sound. There are thousands of nouns in English that end with the ...*tion* sound.

Practice these words:

Two Syllables	Three Syllables	Four Syllables	Five Syllables
Mission	Instruction	Situation	Refrigeration
Nation	Creation	Distribution	Premeditation

Fill in the Blank:

Proverbs 16:23-24 Old Testament

[23] A wise _____ heart guides his mouth, and his _____ promote instruction.

[24] Pleasant words are a _____, sweet to the soul and _____ to the _____ .

[23] A wise man's _____ guides his _____, and his lips promote _____.

_____ words are a honeycomb,

sweet to the _____ and healing to the bones.

Suggested Songs

The Joy of the Lord Is My Strength
God Is So Good

Proverbs 17:1 & 22

¹Better a dry crust with peace and quiet than a house full of feasting, with strife.

²²A cheerful heart is good medicine, but a crushed spirit dries up the bones.

Applicable Linking Rules

Rule #1. Use the (y) glide here. *Quiet= Qui* $^{(y)}$*et*

Flap /d/ rule with better = (be/d/er)

Rule #4. When a word ends in a consonant sound and the next word begins with the same consonant sound, the sound is elongated, but never produced twice and no extra filler sound is used. Example: Crushed spirit. Here crushed is an adjective. The/t/ sound in the single word crushed becomes silent in crushed spirit.

The Rhythm of the Language

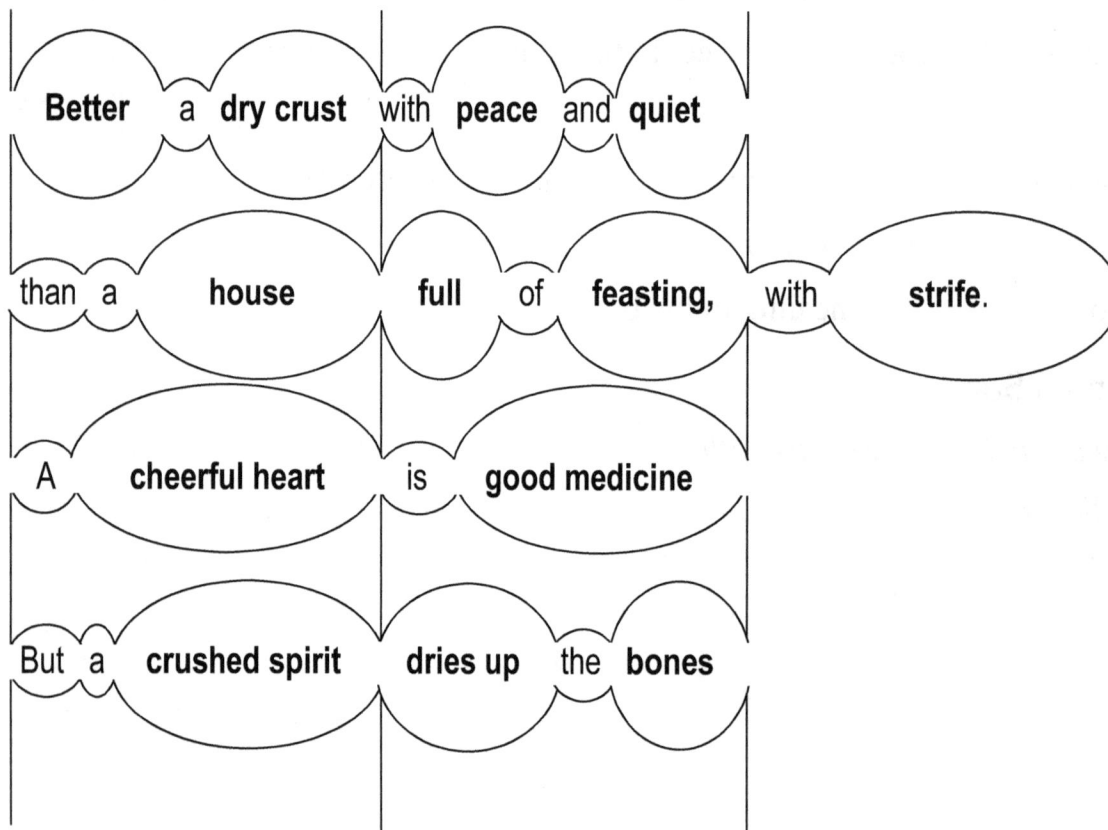

Better   a dry crust with peace and quiet

than a   house   full   of   feasting,   with   strife.

A   cheerful heart   is   good medicine

But a   crushed spirit   dries up   the bones

Bible Verse Chant

Form two groups. Chant each line and read the verse. Repeat as many times as needed. At first, chant slowly, then speed up to normal speaking rate. Finally, work on English voice quality.

Group 1	Group 2
Better a **dry crust** with **peace** and **quiet**	than a **house full** of **feasting**, with **strife**.
A **cheerful heart** is **good** medicine,	but a **crushed spirit dries up** the **bones**.

Groups 1 & 2

[1]**Better** a **dry crust** / with **peace** and **quiet**
than a **house full** of **feasting**, / with **strife**.

[22]A **cheerful heart** is **good medicine**, /
but a **crushed spirit** / **dries up** the **bones**.

Proverbs 17:1 & 22

Vocabulary and Related Words

Adjective	Noun	Verb
Crusty	Crust	To crust (over)
	Feast	To feast
	Strife	To strive

1. Crust: a thin outer coating of bread or pastry; also the thin outer layer of earth; the outer coating of something. Many picky children won't eat the crust on their sandwich. Oxidation forms a crust of rust on cars and metals.

2. Feast: a great meal; a formal extravagant party. Thanksgiving is our feast day.

3. Strife: trouble, fighting, discord. To strive: to try hard to achieve or get something. To do your best. I am uncomfortable in that place because of the constant strife between the children.

Opposites

peace and quiet   strife
a cheerful heart   a crushed spirit

Teacher Notes

Many students have a problem with the long e /iy/. They substitute /i/ as in sheep/ship. In this Bible Verse chant, we have the words *peace* and *feasting*.

Here are some practice minimal pairs. Use a rubber band with this practice exercise. Pull the rubber band and exaggerate the long e sounds until the students are laughing and trying to do the same. Sometimes I write a word like *sheet* on the board with the *e* repeated 6 or more times (*Sheeeeeet*). They get the idea to hold those e sounds a very long time—just right in English.

Minimal Pairs

Sheep	Ship
Beat	Bit
Lead	Lid
Peach	Pitch

Neat	Knit
We'll	Will
Seat	Sit
Reach	Rich

Feet	Fit
Heel	Hill
Each	Itch
Heat	Hit

Long E Practice
Peace
Beach
Sheet

Fill in the Blanks

[1]Better a _____ crust with _____ and quiet than a ____ full of feasting, ____ strife.

[22]A _____ heart is _____ medicine, but a crushed _____ dries up the bones.

——— a dry crust _____ peace and _____ than a house _____ of feasting, with _____.

[22]A cheerful _____ is good medicine, but a _____ spirit dries _____ the bones.

Song Suggestions

Whisper A Prayer

Do Lord

Proverbs 19:2-3

[2]*It is not good to have zeal without knowledge, nor to be hasty and miss the way.*

[3]*A man's own folly ruins his life, yet his heart rages against the Lord.*

Applicable Linking Rules

Rule #1. Use the (y) glide here. *Zeal= ze* [(y)]*al; ruins= ru* [(w)]*ins;*

The Rhythm of the Language

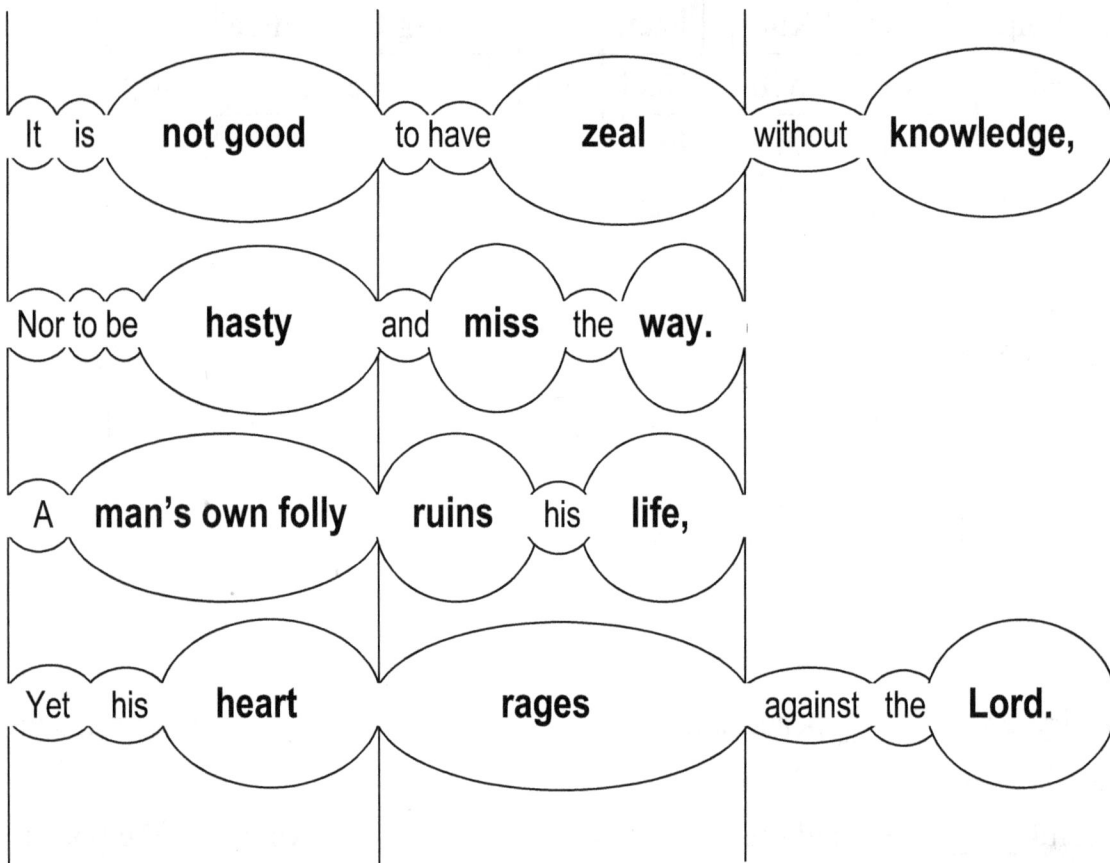

It is **not good** to have **zeal** without **knowledge,**

Nor to be **hasty** and **miss** the **way.**

A **man's own folly** **ruins** his **life,**

Yet his **heart** **rages** against the **Lord.**

Bible Verse Chant

Form two groups. Chant each line and read the verse. Repeat as many times as needed. At first, chant slowly, then speed up to normal speaking rate. Finally, work on English voice quality.

Group 1	*Group 2*
It is **not good** to have **zeal** without **knowledge**,	nor to be **hasty** and **miss** the **way**.
A **man's own folly ruins** his **life**,	yet his **heart rages** against the **Lord**.

Groups 1 & 2
²It is **not good** to have **zeal** without **knowledge**, nor to be **hasty** and **miss** the **way**. ³A **man's own folly ruins** his **life**, yet his **heart rages** against the **Lord**. Proverbs 19:2-3

Vocabulary and Related Words

Adjective	Noun	Verb	Adverb
Zealous	Zeal Zealot		Zealously
Hasty			Hastily
	Miss	To miss	
	Folly		

1. Zeal: energetic and unflagging enthusiasm, especially for a cause or idea. The zealots around Jesus wanted him to destroy the Romans. He plays basketball with such zeal. The zealous lover bought too many flowers.

2. Hasty: done in a hurry, often without thinking or planning. She was so hasty in leaving the store that she left her purse.

3. To Miss: This verb has many meanings: To not see, hear or understand; to fail to be somewhere; fail to do or achieve something. Don't miss the test.

4. Folly: Thoughtless or reckless behavior. Not thinking. It is folly to eat out without having the money to pay.

Teacher Notes:

Many students have a problem with the Voiceless *s* and the Voiced *z*. Have students place their hand on their own throat, above the larynx or voice box. Call it the *Adam's apple* if you like. The teacher should model this to show how it is done. Begin with the /s/, holding the /s/ sound, then switch to the /z/ sound. The teacher and the student should immediately feel the movement of the larynx, and the voicing of the /z/. Be sure to insist your students use their hand on the larynx with this practice exercise.

Minimal pairs

/z/	/s/
Zeal	Seal
Hazy	Hasty
Gains	Against

/z/	/s/
Peas	Peace
Buzz	Bus
Razor	Racer

/z/	/s/
Miz	Miss
Zing	Sing
Rages	Races

/z/ Sounds
Man's own
It is. /idiz/
Ruins

Fill in the Blank

[2]It is _____ good to have zeal without _____, nor to be hasty and _____ the way.

[3]A man's own _____ ruins his life yet his _____ rages against the Lord.

[2]It is not good to _____ zeal without knowledge, nor to _____ hasty and miss the way.

[3] _____ man's own folly ruins his _____, yet his anger rages against _____ Lord

Suggested Song

Only Trust Him

Do Lord

Proverbs 20:11 and 22:6

^{20:11}*Even a child is known by his actions, by whether his conduct is pure and right.*

^{22:6}*Train a child in the way he should go, and when he is old he will not turn from it.*

Structure Words

Structure words, like pronouns, articles, conjunctions, and prepositions are said very quickly and are shortened to fit into the 0.6 sec. sound unit. Practice saying: *and when he is* and *by whether his* and *from it.* Be sure to link all the words together.

The Rhythm of the Language

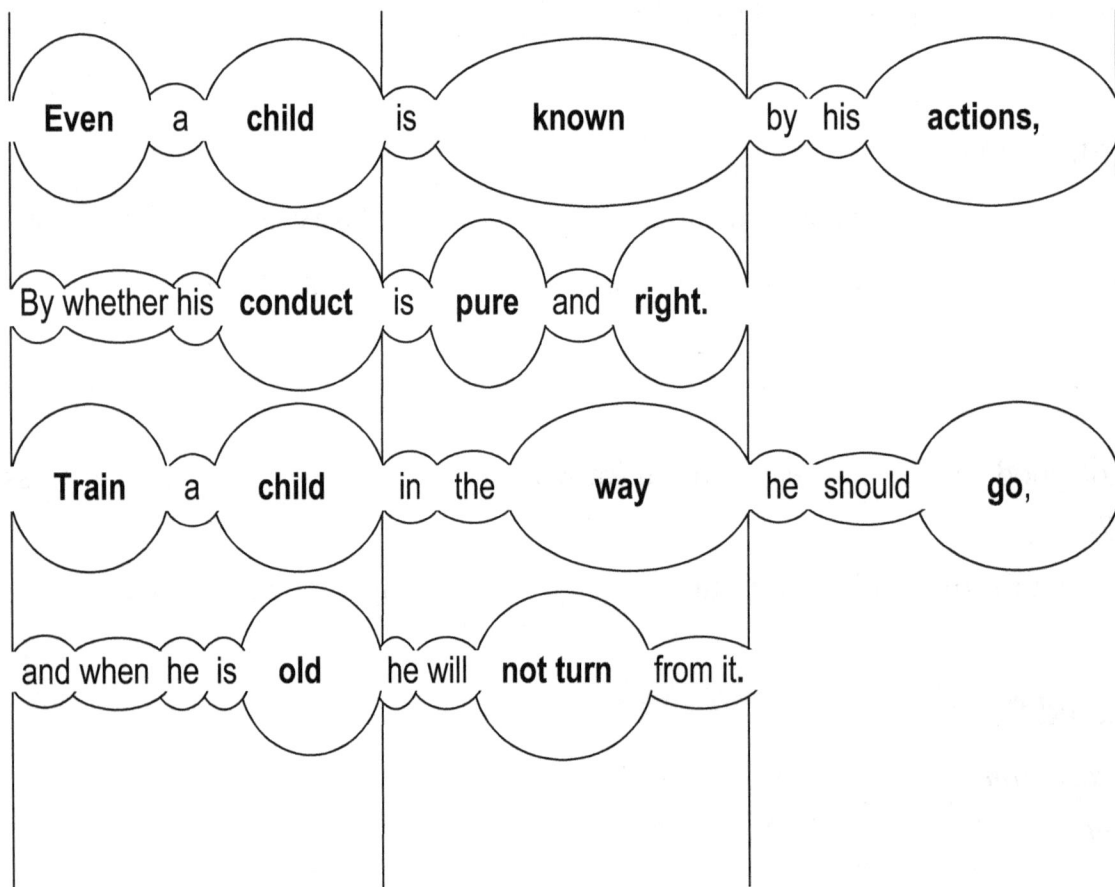

Even a child is known by his actions,

By whether his conduct is pure and right.

Train a child in the way he should go,

and when he is old he will not turn from it.

Bible Verse Chant

Form two groups. Chant each line and read the verse. Repeat as many times as needed. At first, chant slowly, then speed up to normal speaking rate. Finally, work on English voice quality.

Group 1	*Group 2*

Even a **child**
    is **known**
    by his **actions,**
	by whether his **conduct**
	    is **pure** and **right.**

Train a **child**
    in the **way**
    he should **go,**
	and when he is **old**
	    he will **not turn**
	    from it.

Groups 1 & 2

[11]**Even** a **child** / is **known** / by his **actions,** / by whether his **conduct** / is **pure** and **right.** /

[6]**Train** a **child** / in the **way** / he should **go,** / and when he is **old** / he will **not turn** / from it.

Proverbs 20:11 and 22:6

Two *If* and *Whether* Grammar Rules

Often *if* and *whether* are interchangeable.

I don't know if I will buy an iPad.

I don't know whether I will buy an iPad.

There are some rules on when to use *whether*. Here are a couple of them:

1. *After* a preposition, use *whether*.

   He will be judged *by whether* his conduct was appropriate.

   The discussion was *on whether* we should drive or take the bus.

2. *Before* an infinitive, use *whether*.

   I can't decide *whether to* write another book or not.

Note: In formal writing, *whether* is often preferred.

Teacher Notes

There are many rules on the use of *if* and *whether*. However, our purpose is to teach the Bible, and to teach English intelligibility and clarity in speaking. Do not get too bogged down in rules.

Fill in the Blanks

[20:11]Even a _____ is known _____ his actions, by _____ his conduct is pure and _____.

[22:6]Train a child in _____ way he _____ go, and when he _____ old he will _____ turn from it.

[20:11]Even _____ child is known by his _____, by whether _____ conduct is pure and right.

[22:6]Train a _____ in the _____ he should go, and when he is old he will not turn from it.

Suggested Songs

This Little Light of Mine

Jesus Loves the Little Children

Proverbs 22:22-23

[22]*Do not exploit the poor because they are poor, and do not crush the needy in court,*

[23]*for the Lord will take up their case and will plunder those who plunder them.*

Structure Words

Structure words, like pronouns, articles, conjunctions, and prepositions are said very quickly and are shortened to fit into the 0.6 sec. sound unit. Practice saying *and when he is* and *by whether his* and *from it*. Be sure to link all the words together.

The Rhythm of the Language

| Do | **not exploit** | the | **poor** | because they are | **poor** |

| and do | **not crush** | the | **needy** | in | **court.** |

| for the | **Lord** | will | **take up** | their | **cause,** |

| and will | **plunder** | those who | **plunder** | them. |

Bible Verse Chant

Form two groups. Chant each line and read the verse. Repeat as many times as needed. At first, chant slowly, then speed up to normal speaking rate. Finally, work on English voice quality.

Group 1	*Group 2*
Do **not exploit** the **poor** because they are **poor**,	And do **not crush** the **needy** in **court**,
for the **Lord** will **take up** their **cause**	and will **plunder** those who **plunder** them.

Groups 1 & 2

[22]Do **not exploit** the **poor** / because they are **poor**, / and do **not crush** the **needy** / in **court**, /

[23]for the **Lord** / will **take up** their **cause**, / and will **plunder** those / who **plunder** them.

Proverbs 22:22-23

to exploit the poor

to plunder

(Google Images)

Vocabulary

1. Exploit: (verb) To take unfair advantage of someone for personal gain. *Don't exploit the immigrant by charging him more money than normal.*

2. Exploitation: (noun) Unfair treatment of someone for personal gain. *The exploitation of children is responsible for child labor laws in this country.*

3. To crush: (verb) to damage or distort an item. *You can crush your drink cans so they take up less room.*

4. Court (noun): a place where a court of law is held. *If you get a ticket for an automobile accident, you might have to go to court.*(Also the playing surface for certain sports. i.e., tennis court, basketball court, etc.)

5. Cause: (noun) a principle or idea that people believe in. *His cause is health insurance for everyone.*

6. To plunder (verb). To rob or steal goods from people especially during war or unrest. *Pirates often plundered ships at sea; now pirates off Somalia hold ships for ransom.*

7. To take up: A two word verb with many meanings. Here God will begin the defense of the poor. *When I am old, I will take up quilting.* I will begin doing something regularly.

Teacher Notes

Pictures make a great deal of difference to the student. Often, I use Google Images to teach vocabulary.

In addition, I encourage the use of bilingual dictionaries to deal with difficult words. Many students keep electronic bilingual dictionaries with them. A quick search takes care of the comprehension, and the teacher can just go on. Watch for the trap of over-reliance on the dictionary. If it causes a problem, ask the class to look up the words as homework. Use the class time for oral production and repetition.

Fill in the Blanks

[22]Do _____ exploit the _____ because they are poor, and _____ not crush the needy _____ court,

[23] _____ the Lord ____ _____ ____ their case and will plunder those who plunder them.

[22]Do not _____ the poor _____ they are poor, and do not _____ the needy in court,

[23]for the _____ will take up their _____ and will plunder those who _____ them.

Suggested Song

Because I Have Been Given Much

This is a favorite of mine. It helps explain why I teach as a volunteer. Use this song to teach some really necessary vocabulary.

Proverbs 25:21-22

²¹*If your enemy is hungry, give him food to eat; if he is thirsty, give him water to drink.*

²²*In doing this, you will heap burning coals on his head, and the Lord will reward you.*

Structure Words

Structure words, like pronouns, articles, conjunctions, and prepositions are said quickly and are shortened to fit into the 0.6 sec. rhythm. Practice saying *and when he is* and *by whether his* and *from it.* Be sure to link all the words together.

The Rhythm of the Language

If your **enemy** is **hungry,**   give him   **food** to **eat;**

if he is   **thirsty,**   give him   **water** to **drink.**

In doing this,

you will **heap burning coals** on his   **head,**

and the **Lord**   will   **reward**   you.

Bible Verse Chant

Form two groups. Chant each line and read the verse. Repeat as many times as needed. At first, chant slowly, then speed up to normal speaking rate. Finally, work on English voice quality.

Group 1	*Group 2*
If your **enemy** is **hungry**, give him **food** to **eat**;	**No!** He is my **enemy!**
if he is **thirsty**, give him **water** to **drink**.	You **gotta** be **kidding!**
Yes! **Obey** the **Lord!**	**Why?** Why do this for an **enemy?**
In doing this, you will **heap burning coals** on his **head**, and the **Lord** will **reward** you.	We must **return good** for **evil.** We must **return good** for **evil.**

Groups 1 & 2
[21]If your **enemy** is **hungry**, give him **food** to **eat**; if he is **thirsty**, give him **water** to **drink**. [22]**In doing this**, you will **heap burning coals** on his **head**, and the **Lord** will **reward** you.

Proverbs 25:21 and 22

Vocabulary

1. Enemy: Someone who wishes to harm you; a hostile nation or power.

2. Exceptions: a person or a thing that does not fit into the general rule. *Christians need to be exceptions when it comes to revenge and hatred.*

3. Burning coals: an idiom meaning that you will cause him to know that you can benefit him and his heart will be touched. His conscience will move him and he will be changed.

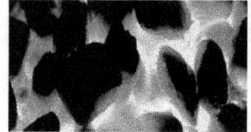

Paul quotes this rule in Romans 12:19-21. Returning good for evil is important.

Teacher Notes

A focal word goes up about a half step in tone, and is held in length like a content word even if it is a structure word. The decision to elevate a word to a focal word is made by a speaker who wants to place emphasis on that word. Using too many focal words is abnormal and makes the speaker sound harsh and shrill.

In this chant, teach, *No! He is my enemy!* Make *no* a focal word, and say it with emphasis and power English. It does not have to be loud at all. Volume can be added to focal words, but it is not necessary. Be sure to have the students go down in tone at the end of the sentences and sound units.

Fill in the Blanks

[21]If _____ enemy is hungry, give him _____ to eat; if he is _____, give him water to drink.

[22]_____ doing this, you will heap _____ coals on his head, and _____ Lord will reward you.

[21]If your enemy is hungry, _____ him food to eat; if _____ is thirsty, give him water _____ drink.

[22]In doing this, you _____ heap burning coals on his _____, and the Lord will reward _____.

Suggested Song

Because I Have Been Given Much

Section 3

Luke 10:25-28

[25]*On one occasion an expert in the law stood up to test Jesus. "Teacher," he asked, "what must I do to inherit eternal life?"*

[26]*"What is written in the Law?" he replied. "How do you read it?"*

[27]*He answered: "Love the Lord your God with all your heart and with all your soul and with all your strength and with all your mind, and 'Love your neighbor as yourself.'"*

[28]*"You have answered correctly," Jesus replied. Do this and you will live."*

Sound Units

Speak or chant in sound units. (Also called breath pauses, and thought groups.)

On one occasion / an expert in the law / stood up to test Jesus. / "Teacher," ↘ / he asked, / "what must I do / to inherit eternal life?" /

"What is written / in the Law?" ↘ / he replied. ↘ / "How do you read it?" ↘ /

He answered: / "Love the Lord your God / with all your heart / and with all your soul / and with all your strength / and with all your mind, / and / 'Love your neighbor / as yourself.'" ↘ /

Applicable Linking Rules

Be sure to link all words in each sound unit.

Rule #3: When a word or syllable ending in a consonant cluster is followed by a word beginning with a vowel, the final consonant is pronounced as if it belongs to both words.

Example: *With all, expert in, must I, strength and*

Rule #4: When a word ends in one consonant and the next word begins with that same consonant sound, the sound is elongated, but never produced twice and no extra filler sound is used.

Example: *eternal life*

Content And Focal words

Content words are **bold**; focal words are **bold underlined**

He **answered:** / "**Love** the **Lord** your **God** / with **all** your **heart** / and with **all** your **soul** / and with **all** your **strength** / and with **all** your **mind**, / **and** / '**Love** your **neighbor** / as **yourself**.'" /

Bible Verse Chant

Form two groups. Chant each line and read the verse. Repeat as many times as needed. At first, chant slowly, then speed up to normal speaking rate. Finally, work on English voice quality.

**Group 1**	_**Group 2**_

Teacher, teacher,
      What must I **do**
      To **inherit Eternal life**?
	What is **written** in the **Law**?
	      How do you **read it**?

**Groups 1 & 2**

Love the **Lord,** your **God**
      with **all** your **heart**
      and with **all** your **soul**
      and with **all** your **strength**
      and with **all** your **mind**.

Heart, Soul, Strength, Mind
      Heart, Soul, Strength, Mind.

And
      love your **neighbor** as **yourself**!

On one **occasion** / an **expert** in the **law** / stood up to test **Jesus**. / "**Teacher**," / he **asked**, / " **what** must I **do** / to **inherit eternal life**?" /

"**What** is **written** / in the **Law**?" / he **replied**. / "**How** do you **read it**?" /

He **answered**: / "**Love** the **Lord** your **God** / with **all** your **heart** / and with **all** your **soul** / and with **all** your **strength** / and with **all** your **mind**, / **and** / 'Love your **neighbor** / as **yourself**.'" /

"You **have answered correctly**," / Jesus replied. / Do **this** / and you will **live**."

Galatians 5:22

²²But the fruit of the spirit is love, joy, peace, patience, kindness, goodness, faithfulness, gentleness and self-control. Against these things, there is no law.

The Rhythm of the Language

English typically has a predetermined rhythm, and the syllables seems to scramble to accommodate this beat. The rhythm requires a major stressed syllable approximately every 0.6 seconds, and there are normally one or two unstressed syllables near each major syllable. (From *Rhythm and Unstress* by Howard B. Woods)

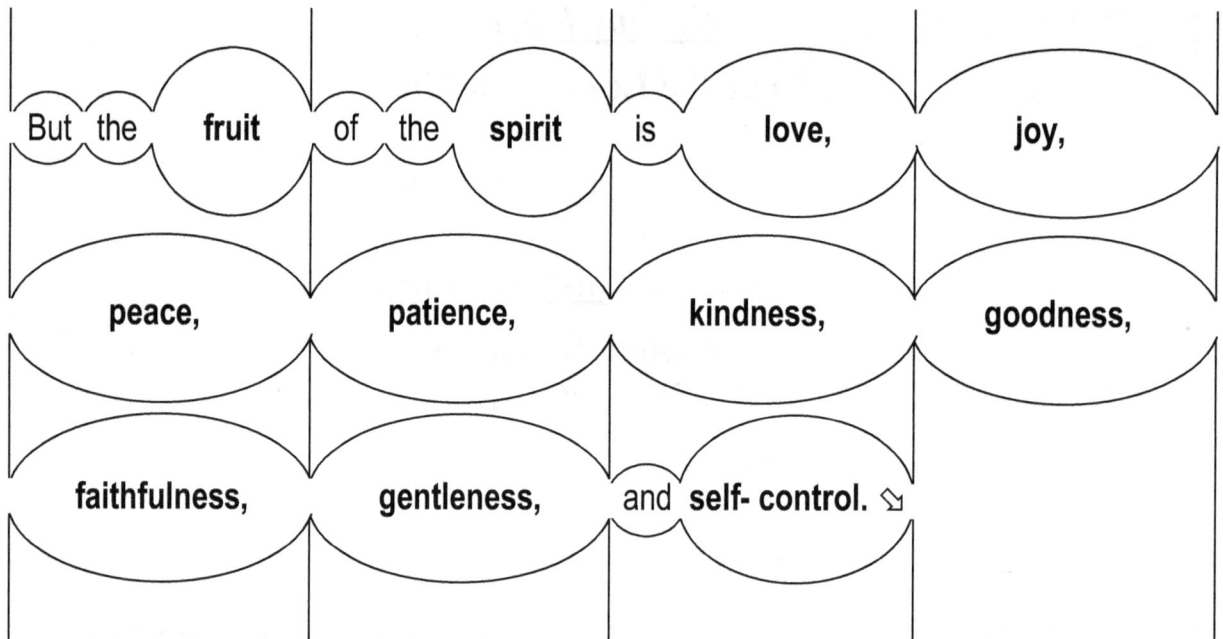

| But the | **fruit** | of | the | **spirit** | is | **love,** | **joy,** |

| **peace,** | **patience,** | **kindness,** | **goodness,** |

| **faithfulness,** | **gentleness,** | and **self- control.** |

Content And Focal words

Content words are **bold**; focal words are **bold underlined**

But the **fruit** / of the **spirit** / is **love,** / **joy,** / **peace,** / **patience,** / **kindness,** / **goodness,** / **faithfulness,** / **gentleness** / and **self-** / **control**. / Against **these** things, / there **is** no **law**.

Bible Verse Chant

Form two groups. Chant each line and read the verse. Repeat as many times as needed. At first, chant slowly, then speed up to normal speaking rate. Finally, work on English voice quality.

Group 1	*Group 2*
Now **faith changes** the **way** we **live**.	**How** does **having faith** do **that**?
God gives us the **Holy Spirit**	**How** do I **recognize** it?
You **see** the **fruit**.	**What** is the **fruit** of the **Holy Spirit**?
But the **fruit** / of the **spirit** / is **love**, / **joy**, / **peace**, / **patience**, / **kindness**, / **goodness**, / **faithfulness**, / **gentleness** / and **self-** / **control**. / Against **these** things, / there **is** no **law**.	But the **fruit** / of the **spirit** / is **love**, / **joy**, / **peace**, / **patience**, / **kindness**, / **goodness**, / **faithfulness**, / **gentleness** / and **self-** / **control**. / Against **these** things, / there **is** no **law**.
So I **say**, **live** by the **Spirit**,	And **you** will not **gratify** the **desires** of the **sinful nature**.

Groups 1 & 2

What is the **fruit** / of the **Holy Spirit**? /

But the **fruit** / of the **spirit** / is **love**, / **joy**, / **peace**, / **patience**, / **kindness**, / **goodness**, / **faithfulness**, / **gentleness** / and **self-** / **control**. / Against **these** things, / there **is** no **law**.

Joshua 1:9

⁹Have I not commanded you? Be strong and courageous. Do not be terrified; do not be discouraged, for the Lord your God will be with you wherever you go.

Applicable Linking Rules

Be sure to link all words in each sound unit.

Rule #5: The stops in English are t, d, p, k, g, and j. When a stop consonant is followed by another stop consonant in the next word, the first stop is not released and that helps the linking. The tongue is in the position but before the air is released the next sound is formed.

Examples: *not commanded, and courageous, not be*

Content And Focal words

Hold each content word one full count. Structure words are one half, one quarter, or one eighth count. Generally the verb *to be* is not a content word.

Content words are **bold**; focal words are **bold underlined**

Have I not **commanded** you? Be **strong** and **courageous**. Do **<u>not</u>** be **terrified**; do **<u>not</u>** be **discouraged**, for the **Lord** your **God** will be with you **wherever** you **go**.

Sound Units

Speak or chant in sound units.

Have I not **commanded** you? ↘ / Be **strong** and **courageous**.↘ / Do **<u>not</u>** be **terrified**; / do **<u>not</u>** be **discouraged**, / for the **Lord** your **God** will be with you / **wherever** you **go**.↘

Backward Build-up

Commanded:	-ded. -manded, commanded
Strong:	-ong, strong
Courageous:	-geous, -rageous, courageous
Discouraged:	-raged, -couraged, discouraged

Bible Verse Chant

Form two groups. Chant each line and read the verse. Repeat as many times as needed. At first, chant slowly, then speed up to normal speaking rate. Finally, work on English voice quality.

Group 1	_Group 2_
Have I not **commanded** you?	Have I not **commanded** you?
Be **strong** and **courageous**.	Be **strong** and **courageous**.
Do **<u>not</u>** be **terrified**;	Do **<u>not</u>** be **terrified**;
do **<u>not</u>** be **discouraged**,	do **<u>not</u>** be **discouraged**,
for the **Lord** — your **God**	for the **Lord** — your **God**
will be with you	will be with you
wherever you **go**.	**wherever** you **go**.

Groups 1 & 2

The **Lord** your **God**
will be with you
wherever you **go**.

Have I not **commanded** you? / Be **strong** and **courageous**. / Do **<u>not</u>** be **terrified**; / do **<u>not</u>** be **discouraged**, / for the **Lord** your **God** will be with you / **wherever** you **go**.

Matthew 7:7-8

[7]*Ask and it will be given to you; seek and you will find; knock and the door will be opened to you.* [8]*For everyone who asks receives; he who seeks finds; and to him who knocks, the door will be opened.*

Applicable Linking Rules

Be sure to link all words in each sound unit.

Linking allows the native speaker to smoothly speak the sound units that make up a sentence. Within a sound unit, all the words go smoothly together with no stops and no extra sounds like 'uh' or 'ah' added.

Rule #2: When a word ending with a single consonant is followed by a word beginning with a vowel, the consonant is held and it sounds like it belongs to both words.

Example: *and it* should sound like */andit/.*

Rule #5: The stops in English are t, d, p, k, g, and j. When a stop consonant is followed by another stop consonant in the next word, the first stop is not released and that helps the linking. The tongue is in the position but before the air is released the next sound is formed.

Example: *and to him* is pronounced as */annto/,* not *and ... to*

Content And Focal words

Hold each content word one full count. Structure words are one half, one quarter, or one eighth count. Generally the verb *to be* is not a content word.

Ask ↘ / and it will be **given** to you; ↘ / **seek** and you will **find**; ↘ / **knock** and the **door** / will be **opened** to you. ↘ / For **everyone** who **asks** / **receives**; / he who **seeks** / **finds**; / and to him who **knocks**, / the **door** will be **opened**. ↘

Structure words need to be spoken quickly.

Example: in the sound unit, *and it will be **given** to you*, the content word, ***given*** receives almost as much time by itself as all of the other words put together.

Note: ↘ *is used as a reminder that the voice goes down at the end of sentences and often at the end of sound units. It is not used every single time, simple as a reminder.*

Bible Verse Chant

Form two groups. Chant each line and read the verse. Repeat as many times as needed. At first, chant slowly, then speed up to normal speaking rate. Finally, work on English voice quality.

Group 1	*Group 2*
Ask! **Ask**! **Ask**! it will be **given** to you.	it will be **given** to you.
Seek! **Seek**! **Seek**! you will **find**.	you will **find**.
Knock! **Knock**! **Knock**! the **door** will be **opened** to you.	the **door** will be **opened** to you.
For **everyone** who **asks** receives;	For **everyone** who **asks** receives;
he who **seeks finds**;	he who **seeks finds**;
and to him who **knocks**	and to him who **knocks**
the **door** will be **opened**.	the **door** will be **opened**.

Groups 1 & 2
For **everyone** who **asks** — **receives**;   and he who **seeks**—**finds**;   and to him who **knocks**—the **door** will be **opened**.

Ask / and it will be **given** to you; / **seek** / and you will **find**; / **knock** / and the **door** will be **opened** to you. / For **everyone** who **asks** / **receives**; / he who **seeks** / **finds**; / and to him who **knocks**, / the **door** will be **opened**.

Romans 5:8

[8]*But God demonstrates his own love for us in this: While we were still sinners, Christ died for us.*

Sound Units

Speak or chant in sound units.

> But God demonstrates
> His own love for us in this:
> While we were still sinners,
> Christ died for us.

Applicable Linking Rules

Be sure to link all words in each sound unit.

Rule #2: When a word ending with a single consonant is followed by a word beginning with a vowel, the consonant is held and it sounds like it belongs to both words.

Examples: *His own* is pronounced */hizown/*; *for us* = */forruss/*.

Rule #4: When a word ends in one consonant and the next word begins with that same consonant sound, the sound is elongated, but never produced twice and no extra filler sound is used.

Example: *God demonstrates*

Rule #5: The stops in English are t, d, p, k, g, and j. When a stop consonant is followed by another stop consonant in the next word, the first stop is not released and that helps the linking. The tongue is in the position but before the air is released the next sound is formed.

Example: *Christ died*

Content And Focal words

Focal words are emphasized and elongated in time: "demonstrates", as a focal word, is spoken in three syllables /dem mon strates/. In this verse, many words can be made into focal words. It is the reader's choice. Here, according to the way you read it, you could choose to emphasize words like, God, His, Us, We, etc.

But **God demonstrates** / his own **love** for **us** / in **this**: / While **we** were still **sinners**, / **Christ died** for us.

Bible Verse Chant

Form two groups. Chant each line and read the verse. Repeat as many times as needed. At first, chant slowly, then speed up to normal speaking rate. Finally, work on English voice quality.

Group 1	***Group 2 (quietly)***
But **God demonstrates**	his own **love** for **us**
But **How?**	In **this**: while **we** were still **sinners**,
Christ <u>died</u> for us.	while **we** were still **sinners**, **Christ <u>died</u>** for us.

Groups 1 & 2
while **we** were still **sinners**,   **Christ <u>died</u>** for us.
But **God demonstrates** / his own **love** for **us** / in **<u>this</u>**: / While **we** were still **sinners**, / **Christ <u>died</u>** for us.

Isaiah 55:11

[11]*So is my word that goes out from my mouth: It will not return to me empty, but will accomplish what I desire and achieve the purpose for which I sent it.*

Applicable Linking Rules

Rule #1: Linking with /y/ or /w/ glides commonly occurs when one word or syllable ends in a tense vowel or diphthong and the next word or syllable begins with a vowel.

Example: *me empty* = *me* [(y)] *empty*

The Rhythm of the Language

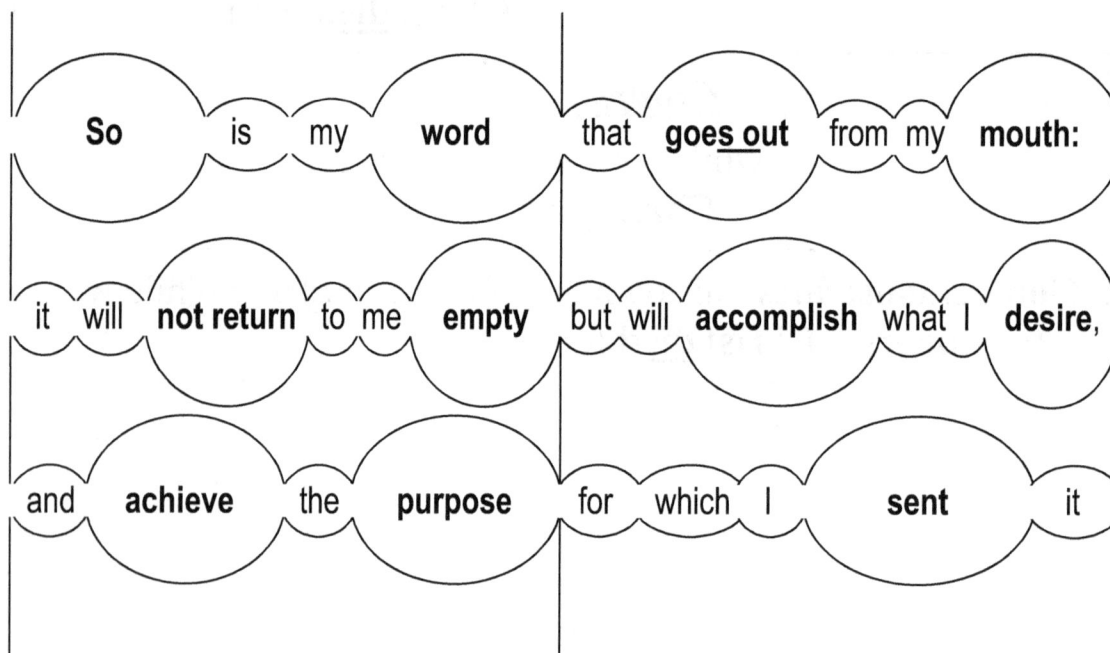

So   is   my   **word**   that   **goes out**   from   my   **mouth:**

it   will   **not return**   to   me   **empty**   but   will   **accomplish**   what   I   **desire,**

and   **achieve**   the   **purpose**   for   which   I   **sent**   it

Sound Units, Content And Focal words

Focal words are emphasized and elongated in time.

> So is my **word** / that **goes out** from my **mouth**: / It will **not return** to me **empty**, / but will **accomplish** / what I **desire** / and **achieve** the **purpose** / for which I **sent** it.

Bible Verse Chant

Form two groups. Chant each line and read the verse. Repeat as many times as needed. At first, chant slowly, then speed up to normal speaking rate. Finally, work on English voice quality.

Group 1	*Group 2 (quietly)*
So is my **word**	that **goes out** from my **mouth**:
It will **not return** to me **empty**	It will **not return** to me **empty**
but will **accomplish**	what I **desire**
and **achieve** the **purpose**	for which I **sent** it.
<div align="center">***Groups 1 & 2*** **What** will **God's word accomplish**? , What **God** wants it to **achieve**!!</div>	
<div align="center">So is my **word** / that **goes out** from my **mouth**: / It will **not return** to me **empty**, / but will **accomplish** / what I **desire** / and **achieve** the **purpose** / for which I **sent** it.</div>	

Daniel 2:20-23

[20]and said: *"Praise be to the name of God for ever and ever; wisdom and power are his. [21]He changes times and seasons; he sets up kings and deposes them. He gives wisdom to the wise and knowledge to the discerning. [22]He reveals deep and hidden things; he knows what lies in darkness, and light dwells with him*

[23]*I thank and praise you, O God of my fathers: you have given me wisdom and power, you have made known to me what we asked of you, you have made known to us the dream of the king."*

Sound Units

Speak or chant in sound units.

Praise be / to the name of God / for ever and ever; / wisdom and power are his. / He changes times and seasons; / he sets up kings / and deposes them. / He reveals deep and hidden things; / he knows / what lies in darkness, / and light dwells with him. /

I thank and praise you, / O God of my fathers.

Applicable Linking Rules

Be sure to link all words in each sound unit.

Rule #2: When a word ending with a single consonant is followed by a word beginning with a vowel, the consonant is held and it sounds like it belongs to both words.

   Examples: *For ever and ever, Wisdom and, sets up, deep and*

Rule #5: The stops in English are t, d, p, k, g, and j. When a stop consonant is followed by another stop consonant in the next word, the first stop is not released and that helps the linking. The tongue is in the position but before the air is released the next sound is formed.

   Examples: *And power, up kings, and disposes, light dwells*

Content And Focal words

"**Praise** be to the **name** of **God** / for **ever** and **ever**; / **wisdom** and **power** are **his**. / He **changes times** and **seasons**; / he **sets up kings** / and **deposes** them. / He **reveals deep** and **hidden things**; / he **knows** / what **lies** in **darkness**, / and **light dwells** with **him**. /

I **thank** and **praise** you, / O **God** / of my **fathers**."

Bible Verse Chant

Form two groups. Chant each line and read the verse. Repeat as many times as needed. At first, chant slowly, then speed up to normal speaking rate. Finally, work on English voice quality.

Group 1	*Group 2*
Praise be to the **name** of **God** for **ever** and **ever**;	**wisdom** and **power** are his.
He **changes times** and **seasons**;	he **sets up kings** and **deposes** them
He **reveals deep** and **hidden** things;	he **knows** what **lies** in **darkness**,
and **light dwells** with **him**.	I **thank** and **praise** you, O **God** of my **fathers**.

Groups 1 & 2
Praise be to the **name** of **God** for **ever** and **ever**; **wisdom** and **power** are **his**.
"**Praise** be to the **name** of **God** / for **ever** and **ever**; / **wisdom** and **power** are **his**. / He **changes times** and **seasons**; / he **sets up kings** / and **deposes** them. / He **reveals deep** and **hidden things**; / he **knows** what **lies** in **darkness**, / and **light dwells** with **him**. /   I **thank** and **praise** you, / O **God** of my **fathers**."

Hebrews 11:1

11Now faith is being sure of what we hope for and certain of what we do not see.

Sound Units

Speak or chant in sound units.

Now faith is being sure / of what we hope for / and certain / of what we do not see.

Grammar note

Two word verb: to <u>hope for</u>

Linking Rules

Be sure to link all words in each sound unit.

Rule #2: When a word ending with a single consonant is followed by a word beginning with a vowel, the consonant is held and it sounds like it belongs to both words.

Example: *fai<u>th is</u>*

Structure words

Prepositions, pronouns, *to be* verb forms, helping or auxiliary verbs, conjunctions, articles, etc. We speak them much quicker.

Examples: *is, of what we, and of what we do*

Content And Focal words

Now **faith** is being **sure** / of what we **hope** for / and **certain** / of what we **do not see.** ↘

Note: ↘ *is used as a reminder that the voice goes down at the end of sentences and often at the end of sound units. It is not used every single time, simple as a reminder.*

Bible Verse Chant

Form two groups. Chant each line and read the verse. Repeat as many times as needed. At first, chant slowly, then speed up to normal speaking rate. Finally, work on English voice quality.

Group 1	*Group 2 (quietly)*
Now **faith** is being **sure**	of what we **hope** for
and **certain**	of what we **do not see**.
What is **faith**?	**Faith** is being **sure** of what we **hope** for.
What **else** is **faith**?	**Faith** is being **certain** of what we **do not see**.
Faith is being **sure** of what we **hope** for, and **certain** of what we **do not see**.	Now, what is **faith**?

Groups 1 & 2
Faith is being **sure** of what we **hope** for, and **certain** of what we **do not see**.
Now **faith** is being **sure** / of what we **hope** for / and **certain** / of what we **do not see**. ↘

Isaiah 58:11

[11]The Lord will guide you always; he will satisfy your needs in a sun-scorched land and he will strengthen your frame. You will be like a well-watered garden, like a spring whose waters never fail.

Comparison

A simile makes a comparison using the words *like* or *as*. Here *like a well-watered garden* means that knowing and depending on God will make you beautiful, productive and strong.

Comprehension and Vocabulary

Words to be defined and explained: scorch, frame, spring.

Structure words

Prepositions, pronouns, *to be* verb forms, helping or auxiliary verbs, conjunctions, articles, etc. We speak them much quicker.

Examples: *and he will*, *you will be like a*

Sound Units, Content And Focal words

The **Lord** will **guide** you <u>**always**</u>; / ↘
he will **satisfy** your **needs** / in a **sun-scorched land** / ↘
and he will **strengthen** your **frame**. / ↘
You will be like a **well-watered garden**, / ↘
like a **spring** / whose **waters** <u>**never fail**</u>. ↘

Note: ↘ *is used as a reminder that the voice goes down at the end of sentences and often at the end of sound units. It is not used every single time, simple as a reminder.*

Bible Verse Chant

Form two groups. Chant each line and read the verse. Repeat as many times as needed. At first, chant slowly, then speed up to normal speaking rate. Finally, work on English voice quality.

**Group 1**	_**Group 2**_
The **Lord** will **guide** you **always**;	he will **satisfy** your **needs** in a **sun-scorched land**
and he will **strengthen** your **frame**	**strengthen** your **frame**

**Groups 1 & 2**	
You will be like a **well-watered garden**, like a **spring** / whose **waters never fail**.	

**Group 1**	_**Group 2 (loud)**_
Who will **guide** me?	The **Lord** will **guide** you!
Who will **satisfy** me?	The **Lord** will **satisfy** you!
Who will **strengthen** my **body**?	The **Lord** will **strengthen** you!

**Groups 1 & 2**	
The **Lord** will **guide** you **always**; / he will **satisfy** your **needs** / in a **sun-scorched land** / And he will **strengthen** your **frame**. / You will be like a **well-watered garden**, / like a **spring** / whose **waters never fail**.	

Joshua 24:15

¹⁵ *" ... then choose for yourselves this day whom you will serve.... But as for me and my house, we will serve the Lord."*

Structure Words

Prepositions, pronouns, *to be* verb forms, helping or auxiliary verbs, conjunctions, articles, etc. We speak them much quicker.

Examples: *whom you will, but as for me and my, we will*

Focal Words

Generally the speaker chooses the focal word to add power to the sentence. Here the speaker can take one or more of the structure words and add power. For example: *whom you will* **serve,** *But as for me / and my* **house**. Which words would you choose? This verse can be used to teach power English.

The Rhythm of the Language

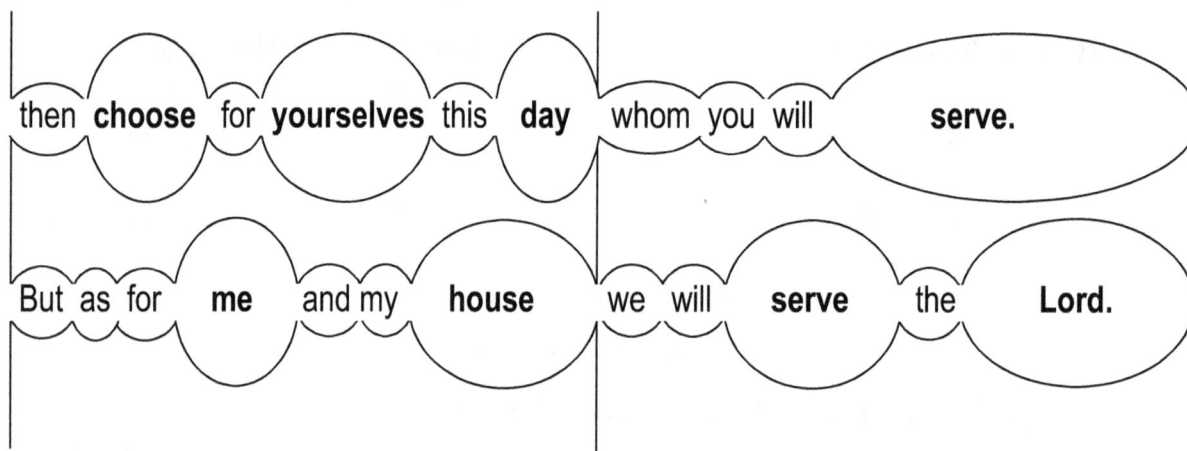

then **choose** for **yourselves** this **day** whom you will **serve.**

But as for **me** and my **house** we will **serve** the **Lord.**

Sound Units And Content Words

then **choose** for <u>yourselves</u> this **day** / whom you will **serve** .... / But as for me and my **house,** / we will **serve** the **Lord."** /

Bible Verse Chant

Form two groups. Chant each line and read the verse. Repeat as many times as needed. At first, chant slowly, then speed up to normal speaking rate. Finally, work on English voice quality.

__Group 1__	*__Group 2__*
then **choose** for **yourselves**	this **day!** this **day!**
whom you will **serve**	whom you will **serve**
But as for me and my **house**	we will **serve** the **Lord!** we will **serve** the **Lord!**

__Groups 1 & 2__	
But as for me and my **house**, / we will **serve** the **Lord**. But as for me and my **house**, / we will **serve** the **Lord**.	

__Group 1__	*__Group 2__*
Who will **choose** the **Lord**?	**I** will **choose** the **Lord**
Who will **you** serve?	**I** will **serve** the **Lord!**

__Groups 1 & 2__	
then **choose** for **yourselves** **this** day / whom you will **serve**.... / But as for **me** and **my** house, / **we** will **serve** the **Lord**.	

1 John 4:7

[7]Dear friends, let us love one another, for love comes from God. Everyone who loves has been born of God and knows God.

Sound Units

Speak or chant in sound units.

> Dear friends,
> let us love one another,
> for love comes from God.
> Everyone who loves
> has been born of God
> and knows God.

Applicable Linking Rules

Be sure to link all words in each sound unit.

Rule #2: When a word ending with a single consonant is followed by a word beginning with a vowel, the consonant is held and it sounds like it belongs to both words.

> Examples: *Let us* = *lettus* or *ledus*
> (flap /d/ rule and the homophone is lettuce)

Rule #5: The stops in English are t, d, p, k, g, and j. When a stop consonant is followed by another stop consonant in the next word, the first stop is not released and that helps the linking. The tongue is in the position but before the air is released the next sound is formed.

> Example: *And knows* (This example has the /d/ and the /k/ stop together.)

Content And Focal words

Dear friends, / let us <u>**love**</u> one another, / for **love** comes from <u>**God**</u>. / Everyone who **loves** / has been **born** of **God** / and **knows God**.

Bible Verse Chant

Form two groups. Chant each line and read the verse. Repeat as many times as needed. At first, chant slowly, then speed up to normal speaking rate. Finally, work on English voice quality.

Group 1	_Group 2 (quietly)_
Dear friends,	let us **love** one another,
for **love** comes from **God**.	Everyone who **loves**
has been **born** of **God**	and **knows God**.
Dear friends, let us **love** one another,	for **love** comes from **God**.
Everyone who **loves**	has been **born** of **God** and **knows God**.

Groups 1 & 2
Let us **love** one another for **love** comes from **God**.

Dear friends, / let us **love** one another, / for **love** comes from **God**. / Everyone who **loves** / has been **born** of **God** / and **knows God**.

Matthew 5:13-16

[13] *"You are the salt of the earth. But if the salt loses its saltiness, how can it be made salty again? It is no longer good for anything, except to be thrown out and trampled by men.*

[14] *"You are the light of the world. A city on a hill cannot be hidden.* [15]*Neither do people light a lamp and put it under a bowl. Instead they put it on its stand, and it gives light to everyone in the house.* [16]*In the same way, let your light shine before men, that they may see your good deeds and praise your father in heaven."*

Applicable Linking Rules

Be sure to link all words in each sound unit.

Rule #1: Linking with /y/ or /w/ glides commonly occurs when one word or syllable ends in a tense vowel or diphthong and the next word or syllable begins with a vowel.

Example: *you* $^{(w)}$*are*

Rule #4: When a word ends in one consonant and the next word begins with that same consonant sound, the sound is elongated, but never produced twice and no extra filler sound is used.

Examples: *its saltiness, good deeds*

Difficult Single Sound

The /th/ sound at the end is difficult.

__Beginning /th/__	__Median /th/__	__Ending /th/__
The, they, thrown	neither, father, anything	earth

Content And Focal words

"You are the **salt** of the **earth**. / But if the **salt** / **loses** its **saltiness**, / **how** can it be made **salty again**? / It is no longer good for **anything**, / except to be **thrown out** / and **trampled** by **men**. /

"You are the **light** / of the **world**. / A **city** on a **hill** / cannot be **hidden**. / Neither do **people** / **light** a **lamp** / and **put it** under a **bowl**. / **Instead** / they **put it** on its **stand**, / and it **gives light** / to **everyone** in the **house**. / In the same way, / let your **light shine** before **men**, / that **they** may **see** your **good deeds** / and **praise** your **father** in **heaven**.

Bible Verse Chant

Form two groups. Chant each line and read the verse. Repeat as many times as needed. At first, chant slowly, then speed up to normal speaking rate. Finally, work on English voice quality.

Group 1	*Group 2*
The **salt** of the earth, **You** are the **salt** of the **earth**.	What if it **loses** its saltiness? How can it be made **salty again**?
Salty **again**? It **can't**. It **can't**. It's no longer good for **anything**.	Except to be **thrown out** and **trampled** by **men**.
The **light** of the **world**. **You** are the **light** of the **world**.	A **city** on a hill cannot be **hidden**.
Neither do **people light** a **lamp** and **put** it under a **bowl**.	**What** do they **do**?
They **put** it on a **stand**,	and it gives **light** to **everyone** in the **house**.
In the same way let your **light shine** before **men**	that they may **see** your good **deeds** and **praise** your **Father** in **heaven**.

Groups 1 & 2

"You are the **salt** of the **earth**. / But if the **salt** / **loses** its **saltiness**, / **how** can it be made **salty again**? / It is no longer good for **anything**, / except to be **thrown out** / and **trampled** by **men**. /

"You are the **light** / of the **world**. / A **city** on a **hill** / cannot be **hidden**. / Neither do **people** / **light** a **lamp** / and **put it** under a **bowl**. / **Instead** / they **put it** on its **stand**, / and it **gives light** / to **everyone** in the **house**. / In the same way, / let your **light shine** before **men**, / that **they** may **see** your **good deeds** / and **praise** your **father** in **heaven**."

Romans 8:28

[28]*And we know that in all things God works for the good of those who love him, who have been called according to his purpose.*

Sound Units

Speak or chant in sound units.

And we know / that in all things / God works / for the good of those / who love him, / who have been called / according to his purpose.

Applicable Linking Rules

Be sure to link all words in each sound unit.

Rule #2: When a word ending with a single consonant is followed by a word beginning with a vowel, the consonant is held and it sounds like it belongs to both words.

Example: *that in* sounds like */tha din/* because the /t/ becomes a flap /d/.

Structure words

Structure words are not held long. Speak them quickly. An easy comparison is that a structure word is like an eighth note in music, and the content word is like a whole note.

Content And Focal words

Focal word to be emphasized: In this verse you could make some structure words into focal words by emphasizing. For example, if you emphasize **his purpose** it means God's and *only* God's purpose.

And we **know** / that in **all things** / **God** works / for the **good** of **those** / who **love** him, / who have been **called** / according to **his purpose**.

Or without those focal words:

And we **know** / that in **all things** / **God works** / for the **good** of **those** / who **love** him, / who have been **called** / according to his **purpose**.

Bible Verse Chant

Form two groups. Chant each line and read the verse. Repeat as many times as needed. At first, chant slowly, then speed up to normal speaking rate. Finally, work on English voice quality.

Group 1	Group 2 (quietly)
And we **know**	Yes, we **know**
that in **all things**	**God works** for the **good**
of **those** who **love** him,	who have been **called** according to his **purpose**.
And we **know**	Yes, we **know**
that in **all things**	**God works** for the **good**
of **those** who **love** him,	who have been **called**

Groups 1 & 2
And we **know** **God works** for the **good** of **those** who **love** him

And we **know** / that in **all things** / **God works** / for the **good** of **those** / who **love** him, / who have been **called** / according to his **purpose**.

Isaiah 40:30-31

[30]*Even youths grow tired and weary, and young men stumble and fall;*

[31]*but those who hope in the Lord will renew their strength. They will soar on wings like eagles; they will run and not grow weary, they will walk and not be faint.*

Applicable Linking Rules

Be sure to link all words in each sound unit.

Rule #2: When a word ending with a single consonant is followed by a word beginning with a vowel, the consonant is held and it sounds like it belongs to both words.

   Examples: *Like eagles, tired and, soar on*

Rule #4: When a word ends in one consonant and the next word begins with that same consonant sound, the sound is elongated – but never produced twice and no extra filler sound is used.

   Examples: *But those,*

Rule #5: The stops in English are t, d, p, k, g, and j. When a stop consonant is followed by another stop consonant in the next word, the first stop is not released and that helps the linking. The tongue is in the position but before the air is released the next sound is formed.

   Examples: *Not grow, not be*

Content And Focal words

Even **youths** grow **tired** and **weary**, /
     and young **men stumble** and **fall**; /
but **those** who **hope** in the **Lord** /
     will **renew** their **strength**. /
They will **soar** on **wings** like **eagles**;
     they will **run** / and not grow **weary**,
     they will **walk** / and not be **faint**.

Bible Verse Chant

Form two groups. Chant each line and read the verse. Repeat as many times as needed. At first, chant slowly, then speed up to normal speaking rate. Finally, work on English voice quality.

Group 1	*Group 2 (quietly)*
Even **youths** grow **tired** and **weary**, **tired** and **weary**	and young **men stumble** and **fall**, **stumble** and **fall**;
but **those** who **hope** in the **Lord** **hope** in the **Lord**	will **renew** their **strength**. their **strength**
They will <u>**soar**</u> on **wings** like **eagles**; **wings** like **eagles**	they will **run** and not grow **weary**, not grow **weary**
they will **walk** and not be **faint**. not be **faint**	they will **walk** and not be **faint**. not be **faint**

Groups 1 & 2
Hope in the **Lord**. **Renew** your **strength** **Soar** like an **eagle** **Don't** grow **weary** **Walk**. **Walk**. **Run**. **Run**.

Even **youths** grow **tired** and **weary**, /
and young **men stumble** and **fall**; /

but **those** who **hope** in the **Lord** /
will **renew** their **strength**. /

They will <u>**soar**</u> on **wings** like **eagles**; /
they will <u>**run**</u> / and not grow **weary**, /
they will <u>**walk**</u> / and not be **faint**.

Jeremiah 33:3

³*Call to me and I will answer you and tell you great and unsearchable things you do not know.*

Sound Units

Speak or chant in sound units.

Call to me / and I will answer you / and tell you great / and unsearchable things / you do not know.

Applicable Linking Rules

Be sure to link all words in each sound unit.

Rule #5: The stops in English are t, d, p, k, g, and j. When a stop consonant is followed by another stop consonant in the next word, the first stop is not released and that helps the linking. The tongue is in the position but before the air is released the next sound is formed.

Examples: *and tell, not know*"

Backward Buildup

Technique: Use the word, "unsearchable." Be sure to hold the primary stress on *un* and *search* with no stress on …*able*. Use the schwa sound of /uh/ with the ending …/uhble/ not …/able/. Use the *Rule of Five* with this.

Imperative Verb

The verb "call" is in the imperative or command tense. It is a *command* for us to obey.

Content And Focal words

Here you could make a structure word into a focal word by emphasizing **to me,** meaning to God. For God is speaking in this verse.

Call to me / and I will **answer** you / and **tell** you **great** / and **unsearchable things** / you **do not know.**

Note: I call Jeremiah 33:3, God's phone number, and I use it a lot.

"What is God's phone number? Does anyone know?"

"It's Jeremiah 33:3, 'Call to me and I will answer you'"

Bible Verse Chant

Form two groups. Chant each line and read the verse. Repeat as many times as needed. At first, chant slowly, then speed up to normal speaking rate. Finally, work on English voice quality.

Group 1	*Group 2*
Call to me	**Call** to me
and I will **answer** you.	and I will **answer** you.
and **tell** you	and **tell** you
great and **unsearchable things**	**great** and **unsearchable things**
You **do not know**.	You **do not know**.
Call to me	**Call** to me
and I will **answer** you.	and I will **answer** you.
and **tell** you	and **tell** you
great and **unsearchable things**	**great** and **unsearchable things**
You **do not know**.	You **do not know**.
Groups 1 & 2	
Call to me, **Call** to me	
Call to me / and I will **answer** you / and **tell** you **great** / and **unsearchable things** / you **do not know.**	

Isaiah 48:17-18

[17]*This is what the Lord says—Your Redeemer, the Holy One of Israel: "I am the Lord your God, who teaches you what is best for you who directs you in the way you should go.*

[18]*If only you had paid attention to my commands, your peace would have been like a river, your righteousness like the waves of the sea."*

Linking Rules

Be sure to link all words in each sound unit.

Rule #2: When a word ending with a single consonant is followed by a word beginning with a vowel, the consonant is held and it sounds like it belongs to both words.

Examples: *This is = thisiz, What is = whadis* (flap /d/ here.)

Rule #4: When a word ends in one consonant and the next word begins with that same consonant sound, the sound is elongated, but never produced twice and no extra filler sound is used.

Examples: *what the, your Redeemer*

Content And Focal words

This is what the **Lord says** — /
Your **Redeemer**, / the **Holy One** of **Israel**: /

"I am the **Lord** your **God**, /
Who **teaches** you / what is **best** for you /
Who **directs** you / in the **way** you should **go**. /

If **only** you had **paid attention** / to my **commands**,
your **peace** would have been / like a **river**, /
your **righteousness** / like the **waves** / of the **sea**."

Bible Verse Chant

Form two groups. Chant each line and read the verse. Repeat as many times as needed. At first, chant slowly, then speed up to normal speaking rate. Finally, work on English voice quality.

Group 1	*Group 2*
This is what the **Lord says** —	Your **Redeemer**, the **Holy One** of **Israel**:
I am the **Lord** your **God**,	Who **teaches** you what is **best** for you
Who **directs** you	in the **way** you should **go**.
If **only** you had **paid attention** to my **commands**,	your **peace** would have been like a **river**, your **righteousness** like the **waves** of the **sea**.

Groups 1 & 2

This is what the **Lord says** — /
    Your **Redeemer**, / the **Holy One** of **Israel**: /
"I am the **Lord** your **God**, /
    Who **teaches** you / what is **best** for you
    Who **directs** you / in the **way** you should **go**.
If **only** you had **paid attention** / to my **commands**,
    your **peace** would have been / like a **river**,
    your **righteousness** / like the **waves** / of the **sea**."

John 3:16

[16] For God so loved the world that he gave his one and only Son that whoever believes in him shall not perish but have eternal life.

Applicable Linking Rules

Be sure to link all words in each sound unit.

Rule #1: Linking with /w/ glides commonly occurs when one word or syllable ends in a tense vowel or diphthong and the next word or syllable begins with a vowel.

Example: *Whoever* becomes *who* [(w)] *ever*

Rule #5: The stops in English are t, d, p, k, g, and j. When a stop consonant is followed by another stop consonant in the next word, the first stop is not released and that helps the linking. This example has the /d/ and the /th/ stop together.

Example: *Loved the*

Difficult to pronounce

The word *world is very difficult for some internationals to say.*

Minimal comparison words

Were, word, world

Content And Focal words

For **God so loved** the **world** / that he **gave** / his **one** and **only Son** / that whoever **believes** in him / shall **not perish** / but have **eternal life.**

Bible Verse Chant

Form two groups. Chant each line and read the verse. Repeat as many times as needed. At first, chant slowly, then speed up to normal speaking rate. Finally, work on English voice quality.

Group 1	*Group 2 (quietly)*
For **God so loved** the **world**	For **God so loved** the **world**
that he **gave**	that he **gave**
his **one** and **only son**	his **one** and **only son**
that whoever **believes** in him shall **not perish** but have **eternal life.**	that whoever **believes** in him shall **not perish** but have **eternal life.**

Groups 1 & 2

For **God so loved** the **world** / that he **gave** / his **one** and **only son** / that whoever **believes** in him / shall **not perish** / but have **eternal life.**

Philippians 4:4-7

[4]*Rejoice in the Lord always. I will say it again: Rejoice!* [5]*Let your gentleness be evident to all. The Lord is near.* [6]*Do not be anxious about anything, but in everything, by prayer and petition, with thanksgiving, present your requests to God.* [7]*And the peace of God, which transcends all understanding, will guard your hearts and your minds in Christ Jesus.*

Applicable Linking Rules

Be sure to link all words in each sound unit.

Rule #1: Linking with /w/ glides commonly occurs when one word or syllable ends in a tense vowel or diphthong and the next word or syllable begins with a vowel.

> Example: *say it = sayit*

Rule #2: When a word ending with a single consonant is followed by a word beginning with a vowel, the consonant is held and it sounds like it belongs to both words.

> Examples: *Rejoice in = rejoicesin, Lord always = Lordalways,*

Rule #4: When a word ends in one consonant and the next word begins with that same consonant sound, the sound is elongated, but never produced twice and no extra filler sound is used.

> Examples: *be evident, with thanksgiving*

Rule #5: The stops in English are t, d, p, k, g, and j. When a stop consonant is followed by another stop consonant in the next word, the first stop is not released and that helps the linking. This example has the /d/ and the /th/ stop together.

> Example: *Not be, and petition, and the, Christ Jesus*

Sound Units, Content And Focal words

Rejoice in the **Lord** **always.** / I will **say it again**: / **Rejoice!** / [5]**Let** your **gentleness** / be **evident** to **all.** / The **Lord** is **near.** / [6]Do **not** be **anxious** about **anything,** / but in **everything,** / by **prayer** and **petition,** / with **thanksgiving,** / **present** your **requests** to **God.** / [7]And the **peace** of **God,** / which **transcends all understanding,** / will **guard** your **hearts** / and your **minds** / in **Christ Jesus.** /

Bible Verse Chant

Form two groups. Chant each line and read the verse. Repeat as many times as needed. At first, chant slowly, then speed up to normal speaking rate. Finally, work on English voice quality.

Group 1	*Group 2*
Rejoice in the **Lord** <u>**always.**</u>	I will **say** <u>it</u> again: **Rejoice!**
Let your **gentleness** be **evident** to **all.**	The **Lord** is **near.**
Do **not** be <u>**anxious**</u> about **anything**	Do **not** be <u>**anxious**</u> about **anything**
but in <u>**everything**</u>,	by **prayer** and **petition**
with <u>**thanksgiving**</u>	with <u>**thanksgiving**</u>
present your **requests** to **God.** which **transcends** **all understanding**	And the **peace** of **God** will **guard** your **hearts** and your **minds**
in **Christ Jesus.**	in **Christ Jesus.**

Groups 1 & 2

Rejoice in the **Lord** <u>**always**</u>.
I will **say** it **again**: <u>**Rejoice!**</u>
[5]**Let** your **gentleness** be **evident** to **all.**
The **Lord** is **near.**

Rejoice in the **Lord** <u>**always.**</u> / I will **say** <u>it</u> again: / **Rejoice!** / [5]**Let** your **gentleness** / be **evident** to **all.** / The **Lord** is **near.** / [6]Do **not** be <u>**anxious**</u> about **anything**, / but in <u>**everything**</u>, / by **prayer** and **petition**, / with <u>**thanksgiving**</u>, / **present** your **requests** to **God.** / [7]And the **peace** of **God**, / which **transcends all understanding**, / will **guard** your **hearts** / and your **minds** / in **Christ Jesus.** /

1 Corinthians 13:4-7

[4]*Love is patient, love is kind. It does not envy, it does not boast, it is not proud.* [5]*It is not rude, it is not self-seeking, it is not easily angered, it keeps no record of wrongs.* [6]*Love does not delight in evil but rejoices with the truth.* [7]*It always protects, always trusts, always hopes, always perseveres.*

Applicable Linking Rules

Be sure to link all words in each sound unit.

Rule #2: When a word ending with a single consonant is followed by a word beginning with a vowel, the consonant is held and it sounds like it belongs to both words.

Examples: *Love is = loviz, delight in = delightin,*

Rule #4: When a word ends in one consonant and the next word begins with that same consonant sound, the sound is elongated, but never produced twice and no extra filler sound is used.

Examples: *with the*

Rule #5: The stops in English are t, d, p, k, g, and j. When a stop consonant is followed by another stop consonant in the next word, the first stop is not released and that helps the linking. This example has the /d/ and the /th/ stop together.

Example: *It does, not boast, not proud, not delight*

The Flap /d/

The /t/ sound takes on a unique quality after a vowel, or an /r/ or an unstressed syllable. The tongue touches the tooth ridge very briefly, like a flap or a tap, and it is voiced.

Example: *not envy =nod envy, it is = id is, not easily = nod easily, it always = id always*

Sound Units, Content And Focal words

[4]**Love** is **patient,** / **love** is **kind.** / It does **not envy,** / it does **not boast,** / it is **not proud.** / [5]It is **not rude,** / it is **not self-seeking,** / it is **not easily angered,** / it **keeps no record** of **wrongs.** / [6]**Love does not delight** in **evil** / but **rejoices** with the **truth.** / [7]It **always protects,** / **always trusts,** / **always hopes,** / **always perseveres.**

Bible Verse Chant

Form two groups. Chant each line and read the verse. Repeat as many times as needed. At first, chant slowly, then speed up to normal speaking rate. Finally, work on English voice quality.

Group 1	_Group 2_
Love is **patient**	**Love** is **kind**.
It does **not envy**	It does **not boast**
Patient. Kind. It is **not proud.** **It is not self-seeking.**	**Not envy! Not boast!** It is **not rude.** It is **not easily angered**
It keeps **no record** of **wrongs**	**No record** of **wrongs** .
Love does not delight in **evil**	But **rejoices** with the **truth**
It <u>**always**</u> **protects**	<u>**always**</u> **trusts**
<u>**always**</u> **hopes**	<u>**always**</u> **perseveres**
Always protects, hopes, trusts, perseveres	**Always protects, hopes, trusts, perseveres**

Groups 1 & 2

Love is **patient**, / **love** is **kind**. / It does **not envy**, / It does **not boast** / it is **not proud**. / It is **not rude**, / it is **not self-seeking**, / it is **not easily angered**, / it **keeps no record** of **wrongs**. / **Love does not delight** in **evil** / but **rejoices** with the **truth**. / It <u>**always**</u> **protects**, / <u>**always**</u> **trusts**, / <u>**always**</u> **hopes**, / <u>**always**</u> **perseveres**.

John 14:1-4

[1]Do not let your hearts be troubled. Trust in God. Trust also in me. [2] In my father's house are many rooms; if it were not so, I would have told you. I am going there to prepare a place for you. [3]And if I go and prepare a place for you, I will come back and take you to be with me that you also may be where I am. [4]You know the way to the place where I am going.

Applicable Linking Rules

Be sure to link all words in each sound unit.

Rule #2: When a word ending with a single consonant is followed by a word beginning with a vowel, the consonant is held and it sounds like it belongs to both words.

> Examples:
> *trust in = trustin*
> *trust also = trustalso*
> *if it = ifit*
> *and if I = andifeye*

Rule #6: When a word ends in a /t/ sound, and the following word is either you, your, or you're, the sounds linked together sound like a /ch/. When a word ends in a /d/ sound, and the following word is either you or your, the sounds linked together sound like a /j/.

> Examples:
> *let your=letchur* or *letchore*
> *that you=thachu* or *thatcha*
> *told you = toldju* or *toldja*

Sound Units, Content And Focal words

Do **not let** your **hearts** be **troubled**. / **Trust** in **God**. / **Trust** <u>also</u> in me. / [2] In my **father's house** / are **many rooms**; / if it were **not** so, / I would have **told** you. / I am **going there** / to **prepare** a **place** for you. / [3]And if I **go** / and **prepare** a **place** for you, / I will **come back** / and **take** you / to **be** with me / that you <u>also</u> / may **be** where I am. / [4]<u>**You**</u> **know** the **way** / to the **place** where <u>**I**</u> am **going**. /

Bible Verse Chant

Form two groups. Chant each line and read the verse. Repeat as many times as needed. At first, chant slowly, then speed up to normal speaking rate. Finally, work on English voice quality.

Group 1	*Group 2*
Do **not let** your **hearts** be **troubled**.	**Trust** in **God**.
Trust <u>also</u> in me.	In my **father's house** are **many rooms**
If it were **not** so, I would have **told** you.	I would have **told** you.
I am **going there**	To **prepare** a **place** for you.
And if I **go** and **prepare** a **place** for you,	I will **come back** and **take** you to **be** with me
That you **<u>also</u>**	May **be** where I am.

Groups 1 & 2

<u>**You**</u> **know** the **way** / to the **place**
where <u>**I**</u> am **going**

John 14:5-7

⁵*Thomas said to him, "Lord, we don't know where you are going, so how can we know the way?"*

⁶*Jesus answered, "I am the way and the truth and the life. No one comes to the Father except through me. ⁷If you really knew me, you would know my Father as well. From now on, you do know him and have seen him."*

Applicable Linking Rules

Be sure to link all words in each sound unit.

Rule #1: Linking with /y/ or /w/ glides commonly occurs when one word or syllable ends in a tense vowel or diphthong and the next word or syllable begins with a vowel.

Examples:
You are is pronounced *you* ^(w)*are*, *now on*=*now* ^(w)*on*, *I am* = *I* ^(y)*am*

Rule #4: When a word ends in one consonant and the next word begins with that same consonant sound, the sound is elongated, but never produced twice and no extra filler sound is used.

Examples: *Thomas said, no one, except through*

Rule #5: The stops in English are t, d, p, k, g, and j. When a stop consonant is followed by another stop consonant in the next word, the first stop is not released and that helps the linking. The tongue is in the position but before the air is released the next sound is formed.

Examples: *would know, said to, don't know*

Sound Units, Content And Focal words

Thomas said to him, / "**Lord**, we **don't know** where you are **going**, so <u>**how**</u> can we **know** the **way**?"

Jesus answered, / "I am the **way** / and the **truth** / and the **life**. / **No one comes** to the **Father** / <u>**except**</u> through me. / If you <u>**really**</u> **knew** me, / you would **know** my **Father** as well. / From now on, you <u>**do**</u> **know** him / and have **seen** him."

Bible Verse Chant

Form two groups. Chant each line and read the verse. Repeat as many times as needed. At first, chant slowly, then speed up to normal speaking rate. Finally, work on English voice quality.

Group 1	*Group 2*
Thomas said to him, "**Lord**, we **don't know** where you are **going**,	so **how** can we **know** the **way**?"
Jesus answered, "I am the **way** and the **truth** and the **life**.	**No one comes** to the **Father** **except** through me.
If you **really knew** me, you would **know** my **Father** as well.	From now on, you **do know** him and have **seen** him."

Groups 1 & 2
The way, the truth and the life!   **The way, the truth and the life!**

Group 1	*Group 2*
Where are you going?	**I'm going with Jesus!**

Groups 1 & 2
He is the way, the truth and the life!

Thomas said to him, / "**Lord**, we **don't know** / where you are **going**, / so **how** can we **know** the **way**?" /
Jesus answered, / "I am the **way** / and the **truth** / and the **life**. / **No one comes** to the **Father** / **except** through me. / If you **really knew** me, / you would **know** my **Father** as well. / From now on, you **do know** him / and have **seen** him."

Psalm 118:1, 24, 28-29

[1] *Give thanks to the Lord, for he is good; his love endures forever.*

[24] *This is the day the Lord has made; let us rejoice and be glad in it.*

[28] *You are my God, and I will give you thanks; you are my God, and I will exalt you.*

[29] *Give thanks to the Lord, for he is good; his love endures forever.*

Applicable Linking Rules

Be sure to link all words in each sound unit.

Rule #6: When a word ends in a /t/ sound, and the following word is either you, your, or you're, the sounds linked together sound like a /ch/. When a word ends in a /d/ sound, and the following word is either you or your, the sounds linked together sound like a /j/.

　Examples: *exalt you = exaltchu*

The Rhythm of the Language

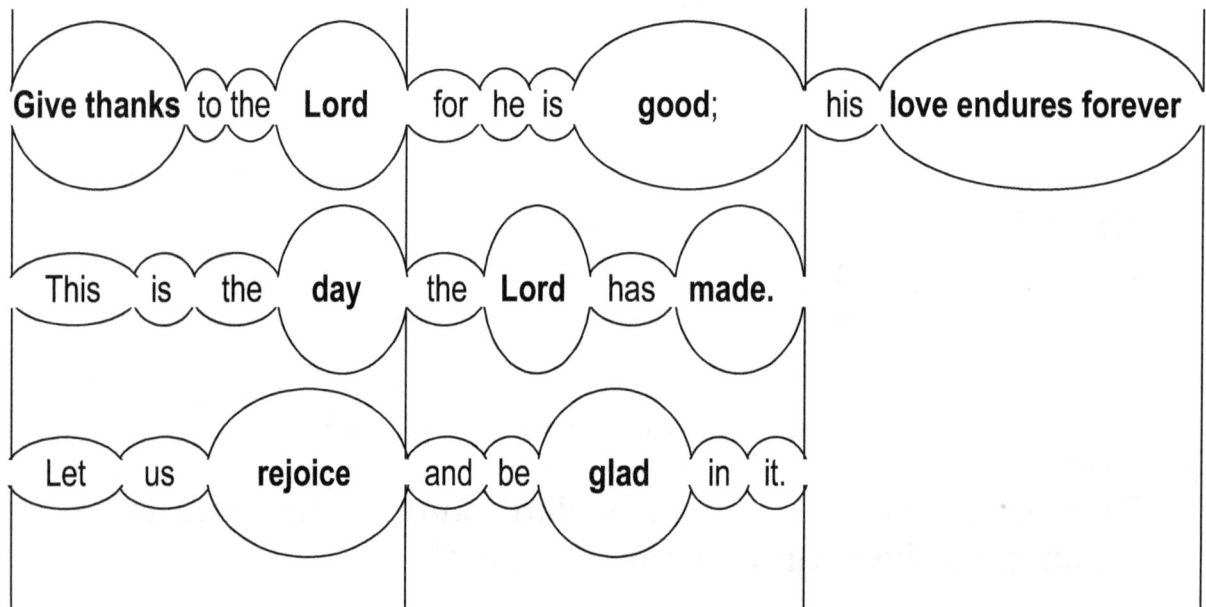

Give thanks to the Lord for he is good; his love endures forever

This is the day the Lord has made.

Let us rejoice and be glad in it.

Bible Verse Chant

Form two groups. Chant each line and read the verse. Repeat as many times as needed. At first, chant slowly, then speed up to normal speaking rate. Finally, work on English voice quality.

Group 1	*Group 2*
Give thanks to the **Lord**	for he is **good**;
his **love endures forever**.	his **love endures forever**.
This is the **day,** This is the **day**	the **Lord** has **made**; the **Lord** has **made**;
let us **rejoice,** let us **rejoice**	and be **glad** in it. and be **glad** in it.
You are __my__ **God,**	and I will **give** you **thanks**;
you are __my__ **God,**	and I will **exalt** you.
Give thanks to the **Lord**	for he is **good**;
his **love endures forever**.	his **love endures forever**.

Groups 1 & 2

Give thanks to the **Lord,** / for he is **good**; / his **love endures forever**. /

This is the **day** / the **Lord** has **made**; / let us **rejoice** / and be **glad** in it. /

You are my **God,** / and I will **give** you **thanks**; / you are my **God,** / and I will **exalt** you. /

Give thanks to the **Lord,** / for he is **good**; / his **love endures forever**.

Matthew 28:18-20

[18]*Then Jesus came to them and said, "All authority in heaven and on earth has been given to me.* [19]*Therefore go and make disciples of all nations, baptizing them in the name of the Father and of the Son and of the Holy Spirit,* [20]*and teaching them to obey everything I have commanded you. And surely I am with you always, to the very end of the age."*

Applicable Linking Rules

Be sure to link all words in each sound unit.

Rule #5: The stops in English are t, d, p, k, g, and j. When a stop consonant is followed by another stop consonant in the next word, the first stop is not released and that helps the linking. This example has the /d/ and the /th/ stop together.

Example: *ma<u>ke</u> <u>d</u>isciples*

Syllables and Backward Buildup

Using your fingers, count the syllables of these words: authority (4), disciples (3), baptizing (3), commanded (3). If necessary, use backward buildup until the class can easily say the words.

World is a very difficult word for many to say. Although it is one syllable, many substitute *word* for *world*. In re-spelling, it would be like /were ul d/. Be sure the students hear all the sound (phonemes) and to use a hand motion to show it is one syllable.

Sound Units, Content And Focal words

Then **Jesus came** to them / and **said,** / "**<u>All</u> authority** in **heaven** / and on **earth** / has been **given** to me. / **Therefore** / **go** and **make disciples** / of **<u>all</u> nations,** / **baptizing** them / in the **name** of the **Father** / and of the **Son** / and of the **Holy Spirit,** / and **teaching** them / to **obey everything** / I have **commanded** you. / And **<u>surely</u>** / I am with you **<u>always</u>,** / to the **very end** of the **age.**" /

Bible Verse Chant

Form two groups. Chant each line and read the verse. Repeat as many times as needed. At first, chant slowly, then speed up to normal speaking rate. Finally, work on English voice quality.

Group 1	**Group 2**
Then **Jesus came** to them and **said**,	"**All authority** in **heaven** and on **earth** has been **given** to me.
Therefore go and **make disciples**	**Disciples** of **all nations**,
baptizing them in the **name** of the **Father**	and of the **Son** and of the **Holy Spirit**,
and **teaching** them to **obey everything**	I have **commanded** you.
And **surely**	I am with you **always**,
to the **very end** of the **age**."	to the **very end** of the **age**."

Groups 1 & 2
And **surely** I am with you **always**,   to the **very end** of the **age**."

Then **Jesus came** to them / and **said**, / "**All authority** in **heaven** / and on **earth** / has been **given** to me. / **Therefore** / **go** and **make disciples** / of **all nations**, / **baptizing** them / in the **name** of the **Father** / and of the **Son** / and of the **Holy Spirit**, / and **teaching** them / to **obey everything** / I have **commanded** you. / And **surely** / I am with you **always**, / to the **very end** of the **age**." /

Matthew 28:18-20

Psalm 23

[1]*The Lord is my shepherd, I shall not be in want.*

[2]*He makes me lie down in green pastures, he leads me beside quiet waters,*

[3]*he restores my soul. He guides me in paths of righteousness for his name's sake.*

[4]*Even though I walk through the valley of the shadow of death, I will fear no evil, for you are with me; your rod and your staff, they comfort me.*

[5]*You prepare a table before me in the presence of my enemies. You anoint my head with oil; my cup overflows.*

[6]*Surely goodness and love will follow me all the days of my life, and I will dwell in the house of the Lord forever.*

Applicable Linking Rules

Be sure to link all words in each sound unit.

Rule #1: Linking with /w/ glides commonly occurs when one word or syllable ends in a tense vowel or diphthong and the next word or syllable begins with a vowel.

> Example: /w/ glide: *no evil = no [(w)]evil*
> /y/ glide: *be in = be [(y)]in, my enemies = my [(y)]enemies*

Rule #2: When a word ending with a single consonant is followed by a word beginning with a vowel, the consonant is held and it sounds like it belongs to both words.

> Example: *Lord is, rod and, with oil, cup overflows*

Rule #4: When a word ends in one consonant and the next word begins with that same consonant sound, the sound is elongated, but never produced twice and no extra filler sound is used.

> Example: *Name's sake*

Psalm 23, King James Version

All together

The Lord is my shepherd; I shall not want.

He maketh me to lie down in green pastures; he leadeth me beside the still waters.

He restoreth my soul: he leadeth me in the paths of righteousness for his name's sake.

Yea, though I walk through the valley of the shadow of death, I will fear no evil; for thou *art* with me; thy rod and thy staff they comfort me.

Thou preparest a table before me in the presence of mine enemies: Thou anointest my head with oil; my cup runneth over.

Surely goodness and mercy shall follow me all the days of my life: and I will dwell in the house of the Lord forever.

133

Psalm 23 New International Version

All together

The Lord is my shepherd,
    I shall not be in want.

He makes me lie down in green pastures,
    he leads me beside quiet waters,
    he restores my soul.

He guides me in paths of righteousness
    for his name's sake.

Even though I walk
    through the valley of the shadow of death,
    I will fear no evil,
    for you are with me;
    your rod and your staff,
    they comfort me.

You prepare a table before me
    in the presence of my enemies.
    You anoint my head with oil;
    my cup overflows.

Surely goodness and love will follow me
    all the days of my life,
    and I will dwell in the house of the Lord
    forever.

Bible Verse Chant

Group 1	Group 2 (quietly)
The Lord is my shepherd, I shall not be in want.	He makes me lie down in green pastures,
he leads me beside quiet waters. he restores my soul.	He guides me in paths of righteousness for his name's sake.
Even though I walk through the valley of the shadow of death,	I will fear no evil, for you are with me; your rod and your staff, they comfort me.
You prepare a table before me in the presence of my enemies.	You anoint my head with oil; my cup overflows.
Surely goodness and love will follow me all the days of my life,	and I will dwell in the house of the Lord forever.

Groups 1 & 2

The **Lord** is my **shepherd**, / I shall not be in **want**. /

He **makes** me **lie down** / in green **pastures**, / he **leads** me beside quiet **waters**, / he **restores** my **soul**. /

He **guides** me / in **paths** of **righteousness** / for his **name's sake**. /

Even though I **walk** / through the **valley** of the **shadow of death**, / I will **fear** no **evil**, / for **you** are with me; / your **rod** and your **staff**, / they **comfort** me.

You **prepare** a **table** before me / in the **presence** of my **enemies**. / You **anoint** my **head** with **oil**; / my **cup overflows**. /

Surely **goodness** and **love** / will **follow** me / all the **days** of my **life**, / and I will **dwell** / in the **house** of the **Lord** / **forever**.

Section 4

Write Your Own Bible Verse Chant

Directions

Use the verses on the following page and write your first four lessons. Here's how:

1. Bible Verse: Include the verse itself in the lesson

2. Linking Rules: Locate *The Linking Rules* in *Basic Concepts and Definitions* on page 9 of this book. Find words in the scripture verse that can illustrate one or two of the rules. Include applicable rules and examples in the lesson.

3. Chant: Write a chant by selecting parts from the verse and separating the parts so that they can be vocalized back and forth by two groups. Include at least one part that will be vocalized by the combined group. Typically the combined part will be at the end. You should always teach the verse as well as using it as a chant. You can *teach* it first or *chant* it first.

4. (optional) The Rhythm of the language: Although using bubbles to show content words is nice, bubbles are difficult and time consuming to produce. You can use other techniques to mark content words such as enclosing them in parentheses, or making them bold. The object is to show that a content word or focal word happens about every 0.6 second; and that content words and focal words are held longer while structure words are spoken quickly.

5. (optional) Content Words and Focal Words: Repeat all or part of the verse and identify the content words and focal words and emphasize them using bold and bold plus underlining respectively. Sound Units: Repeat the verse and mark between the sound units with a forward slash. Use short sound units for beginners, and use longer sound units for more advanced students.

6. (optional) Vocabulary Expansion: Use words or phrases from the verse.

7. (optional) Single Sounds: Select single sounds from the verse.

8. (optional) Fill In The Blanks: Present all or part of the verse as a fill in the blanks game. Always present the same text twice with different words missing.

9. Teachers Notes: Provide additional information that will assist in the lesson.

The point in doing a verse many different ways is to get enough repetition without becoming boring; however you still need to repeat *each part* of the lesson multiple times. You may choose to go over one part a few times and move to the next part; other times you may decide to go through the entire lesson and then repeat all of it. Just mix it up based on the level of your students and the content of the lesson.

Here are your four verses:

2 Timothy 1:7

For God did not give us a spirit of timidity, but a spirit of power, of love, and of self-discipline.

Titus 2:7

In everything set them an example by doing what is good. In your teaching show integrity, seriousness and soundness of speech that cannot be condemned so that those who oppose you may be ashamed because they have nothing bad to say about us.

Isaiah 43:1-2

... I have called you by name; you are mine. When you pass through the waters, I will be with you, and when you pass through the rivers they will not sweep over you. When you walk through the fire, you will not be burned; the flames will not set you ablaze, for I am the Lord, your God.

Jonah 2:9

But I, with a song of Thanksgiving, will sacrifice to you. What I have vowed, I will make good. Salvation comes from the Lord.

Bibliography

Celce-Murcia, Marianne, Donna M. Brinton, and Janet Goodwin. *Teaching Pronunciation, A Reference for TESOL.* Cambridge University Press. 1996.

Clarey and Dixon. *Pronunciation Exercises in English.* Regents Publishing Co. 1963.

Gilbert, Judy. *Clear Speech.* Cambridge University Press, 2nd Ed. 1984-1995.

Gilbert, Judy. *Clear Speech.* Cambridge University Press, 3rdd Ed. 2005.

Graham, Carolyn. *Jazz Chants.* Oxford University Press. 1978.

Graham, Carolyn. *Jazz Chants.* Oxford University Press. 1986.

Graham, Carolyn. *Grammarchantss.* Oxford University Press. 1993

Nilsen and Nilsen. *Pronunciation Contrasts in English.* Regents Publishing Co. 1971, 1973.

Woods, Howard B. *Rhythm and Unstress.* About 1972. Available from Government of Canada Publications (http://publications.gc.ca/site/eng/270779/publication.html). Companion audio tape also available (http://publications.gc.ca/site/eng/237527/publication.html).

Wong, Linda. *Essential Study Skills, Third Edition.* Boston. Houghton Mifflin. 2000.

Weinstein, Nina. *Whaddayasay?* Guided Practice in Relaxed English. 2nd ed. Prentice Hall Regents. ISBN0-201-670-40-2

About The Author

Glenda Reece has been a teacher, a trainer, an author, and a content creator for ESL and Cross Culture programs from Alaska to Florida; and has trained foreign speaking ESL teachers in China and South America. Her work has ranged from the North Carolina Governor's committee for refugee resettlement to high school ESL teacher to business owner to Literacy volunteer.

She has taught or led seminars for the Immigration and Refugee Center, the National Association of Foreign Student Advisors (NAFSA), Teachers of English to Speakers of Other Languages (TESOL), Southeastern Seminary, North Carolina State University, the University of North Carolina, Duke University, Wake County School System, and at Literacy Conferences for Baptist State Conventions in numerous states.

Glenda is the owner of ESL Training Service, which provides English and Cross Cultural training to international business professionals in the Raleigh, NC, area. She was an early president of the North and South Carolina chapter of TESOL. She has been recognized by the Baptist State Convention of North Carolina as Literacy Volunteer of the Year, and was presented the Mildred Blankenship National Volunteer of the Year Award by the North American Mission Board of the Southern Baptist Convention.

She is the author of a two-volume ESL textbook, *English Lessons from the Bible: The Book of Mark*. Student and Teacher versions of these books, which have been in continuous publication since 1989, are available at Lifeway.com. They are sold at cost and without royalties to the author. The books have been used in programs, both Christian and secular, in every corner of the globe.

Glenda has produced several training videos including *Conversational English Using the Lipson Method, The Oral Interview Procedure,* and *Getting Serious About Top-Down and Bottom-Up Pronunciation.*